THE ROOKIE'S PLAYBOOK

Insights and Dirt for New Principals

Autumn Tooms

ScarecrowEducation
Lanham, Maryland • Toronto • Oxford
2005

Published in the United States of America
by ScarecrowEducation
An imprint of the Rowman & Littlefield Publishing Group, Inc.
4501 Forbes Boulevard, Suite 200, Lanham, Maryland 20706
www.scarecroweducation.com

PO Box 317
Oxford
OX2 9RU, UK

British Library Cataloguing in Publication Information Available

Library of Congress Cataloging-in-Publication Data

Tooms, Autumn, 1965–
  The rookie's playbook : insights and dirt for new principals / Autumn Tooms.
      p. cm.
  Includes bibliographical references and index.
  ISBN 1-57886-184-5 (pbk. : alk. paper)
 1. First year school principals. 2. School administrators. 3. Educational
leadership. 4. School management and organization. I. Title.
LB2831.6.T66 2005
371.2'012—dc22

2004014231

⊗™The paper used in this publication meets the minimum requirements of
American National Standard for Information Sciences—Permanence of
Paper for Printed Library Materials, ANSI/NISO Z39.48-1992.
Manufactured in the United States of America.

CONTENTS

ACKNOWLEDGMENTS

This book is the result of a series of conversations with graduate students, aspiring administrators, new and veteran principals, and professors from various universities. It also grew from lessons learned in my own professional career.

I was fortunate to have the cheerful assistance of Jennifer Rogers who was a delight to work with. My Editors, Cindy Tursman and Nicole Carty, were patient with my many questions and cheerleaders from the beginning. I would like to thank Bob Christy for his exceptional photography and Eve Dalton for her intensive graphic design and layout efforts. Both have a keen eye and understand how to translate theoretical concepts into witty and wry images. I would be absolutely neglectful if I failed to mention the inspiration and support of Kitty Sulley. She believed in me more than once and I am forever grateful.

There are three professionals whose contributions demand my further recognition. They are Dr. Robert Stout, Dr. Gwen Glaseman-Worthington, and Dr. Robert Mosby. They are the greatest teachers I know; all three supported me through my development as a thinker, teacher, and leader. Specifically, Dr. Stout showed me the power of carefully listening to, and telling, people's stories. Dr. Glaseman-Worthington modeled for me the importance of balance. And Dr.

Mosby, the only shaman I ever met, proved that dragons can be slayed. I am forever greatful for their generous gifts.

The teacher who had the most profound impact on me was Captain Leighton Tooms. He was a dedicated humanitarian with a keen sense of politics. Furthermore, he was a wonderful daddy. *The Rookie's Playbook: Insights and Dirt for New Principals* is dedicated to his memory.

READER'S NOTE

The Rookie's Playbook: Insights and Dirt for New Principals was written by a former school principal for you, the practicing principal who is new to the position. However, this book is also intended to remind superintendents, teacher leaders, and mentor principals of the perspective that new principals have and provide them with ideas and discussion points.

This book can be digested in one afternoon, or it can be inhaled a few minutes at a time over a quick cup of coffee. You do not have to read this book from the first chapter in order to the last chapter. If you are a busy reader with minimal time, go directly to the chapter that interests you and look for the "instant replay" section. There you will find the specific suggestions discussed in the previous pages. If you have a little more time, flip through the chapters and review the information highlighted in the graphics that resemble post-it notes.

If you have a bigger chunk of time available, read a chapter from the beginning, which starts with a real-life experience shared by one of your colleagues. While the events and leadership recollections described are true, some of the names of the administrators have been changed in accordance with the wishes of those involved with this book. Above all, this effort is meant to be an enjoyable and informative one intended to welcome you to one of the most invigorating and challenging positions in the field of education: the principalship.

1

PRINCIPAL'S OFFICE

WELCOME
TO THE
BIG LEAGUES

Susan Stevens walked nervously down the hall to the assistant principal's office. It was a typically warm April day at Central High School and
she had just started to feel good about her first year as an English
teacher. While Susan knew she had done nothing wrong, being sum-
moned to Mr. Martin's office made her feel like a sophomore who had
been caught kissing in the hallway. Susan found Hugo Martin, Central's
chief disciplinarian, waiting for her with a warm smile. "Hiya, Kiddo!
Come on in. Can I get you a soda or something?" Instead of addressing
his question, Susan could not help but blurt out, "Why did you call me
up here?"

Mr. Martin recognized Susan's insecurities and quickly assured her
that she had done nothing wrong. In fact, he believed Susan was one of
the best teachers on Central's staff. She was polite, always had a smile
on her face, and regularly volunteered to help with campus events. Susan had quickly become one of the most popular teachers at Central because of her creativity in the classroom. Students loved her. The faculty
saw her as a breath of fresh air and parents respected her. That is why it
was all the more difficult for Central's assistant principal to have to explain what the phrase *Reduction in Force* meant. Mr. Martin had to tell
one of his favorite colleagues that she did not have a position on staff for
the following year. Not because she was a bad teacher, but because she
had the least seniority of all the teachers in her department.

He took a deep breath and said, "Susan, I think I can bring you back
on staff next fall. I just can't guarantee you a contract yet. Negotiations
with the teachers' union are not finished and the staffing projections are
incomplete. You are a wonderful teacher and we need you here."

"But Mr. Martin, I need a job. I support myself and I have to be able
to pay my bills. When will you be able to offer me a contract? When will
I know if I really get to come back to Central High School?"

"We will know something by the end of the summer. I realize this
seems like a long time to not know about your future, but staffing is a
slow process that I really don't have much control over. I promise I will
do everything I can to get you back here at Central. If you like, you can
check on our progress during the summer. I hope you can trust me. Our
kids need you, and I won't let you down. Right now, though, I am only
80 percent sure I can guarantee you a job next year. I know I can get this
worked out for you. You'll just have to have a little faith in me."

So Susan put her faith in Mr. Martin. And she tried not to worry when she heard her colleagues talk about their plans for the summer and for the following year. She taught summer school at North High School to make money and she called Central High once a week during June and July to see if she had a job. Every time Susan called, Mr. Martin said he was working on it. When August rolled around, Susan was scared. She had passed up opportunities to teach at other schools because she really wanted to stay at Central. While the other teachers were going back to campus to set up their classrooms, Susan checked her answering machine to find no phone calls from Mr. Martin.

Then, on the day before students were to report to class, Mr. Martin called Susan and told her he had found a way to offer her a contract. That fall, Susan taught English, study hall, and yearbook. She sponsored student government and worked dances. Susan contributed to her campus in any way she could and she never complained. Susan only remembered that Hugo Martin kept his word.

Ten years and a national teaching award later, Susan Stevens is once again the rookie at a new school. However, this time she is walking down the hall on a warm April day reflecting on her first year as the principal. She thinks about how it is her turn to make promises to teachers and to ask them to have faith in her. Occasionally, when Susan is asked why she left a successful career in the classroom to become a school administrator she tells the story of her first year as a teacher and the promise Mr. Martin kept. She talks about how she admired Mr. Martin for more than his ability to keep his word. She admired his loyalty to their principal, Dave Silcox. She also noticed how he had this way of getting things done at Central High School. While Hugo was an ardent teacher advocate, he made clear his expectations for excellence in the classroom. Hugo could be as formidable as he was compassionate. When he was confronted with complaints about tough decisions he made, he would simply state that all of his actions were in the best interest of students. He was not wildly charismatic but his greatness as a leader rested in his integrity, loyalty, and dedication to the Central High School community.

When Susan completed graduate school, she invested time in talking to Mr. Martin about his views concerning school leadership. Those conversations helped her to develop her own sense of what effective

leaders do. When the time was right, she accepted her first administrative position as an assistant principal at another high school across
town. Like most conscientious protégés, Susan continued to call Mr.
Martin for mentorship during her tenure as an assistant.

After five years as an assistant, Susan began to interview for principal positions. When she was selected as the principal of Bells High
School, the first person Susan called was Hugo Martin. She could not
wait to share the good news of her promotion and to ask for words of
wisdom. However, Susan was a little surprised at his reaction. Hugo
was naturally thrilled for her achievement but gently added, "You
know, Kiddo, being a principal is a whole different ball game than being the assistant principal. I think you need more than my perspective
at this point. I think you need to talk to someone who has been there.
I think you need to call Dave." So she had a very long conversation
with Dave Silcox. They talked about leadership, politics, and what it
means to be the curriculum leader of a school. When the conversation
ended, Susan discovered suddenly that she was more than a little intimidated about her new position. Why? Because it was beginning to
look as if the principalship was a completely different job than the assistant principalship.

Now, eight months after that long conversation about leadership, the
April sun reminded Susan that despite her five years of experience as an
assistant, and a Ph.D. in educational administration, Dave's insights
were absolutely correct. Entering the principalship is like being shipped
up to the big leagues. Like it or not, this world was completely different
than what she had known before.

THE PRINCIPALSHIP IS NOTHING
LIKE THE ASSISTANT PRINCIPALSHIP

What distinguishes principals from other leaders is that they are single-
handedly held accountable for everything that happens at their school.
Whether or not the principal has control of a situation is irrelevant. For
example, it is assumed by everyone that you are responsible for all the
rules and practices at your school. Georgia Combs, a principal in Scotts-
dale, Arizona, remembers:

My school is unique in that it was built at the end of a small street—therefore it only had one car entrance on the south side of campus for student drop off. The quiet neighborhood street that bordered the north side of our baseball fields had a gate that we opened in the morning to allow children who walked to school on campus. Parents in a hurry began to drop their kids off on the street by the gate in order to avoid the huge traffic jam in our parking lot. One of our neighbors, Mr. Jones, was weary of the increasing street traffic at the baseball field gate. He demanded that I lock it in order to restore peace and quiet to his street. I informed him that our participatory management team would have to discuss that issue and invited him to our next meeting. Mr. Jones did not attend the meeting. The team, consisting of teachers and parents in the neighborhood, voted to keep the gates open. I called Mr. Jones after the meeting to inform him that the gates would have to stay open. He was furious. He could not understand that I had no power to lock the gates. Can you guess what happened next? Yep, Mr. Jones called my superintendent. He next called a couple of governing board members and spoke at a board meeting. Finally, he called the local police precinct—and then the mayor's office. Naturally, all of these people called me. Because no one could give him the answer he wanted, Mr. Jones continued to call all of the people mentioned above *every month*. Those folks then called me every month. This dance of frustration got to the point where my assistant superintendent told me, "I want you to make this problem go away, we are all exhausted with this guy."

I did not know how to make it go away. I asked my leadership team for help. They did not know how to make it go away. No one at the district office or the mayor's office knew how to make it go away. I felt horrible. One of the unwritten rules is that principals are supposed to keep complaints from going to the district office. I felt that I had let them down because I could not solve this problem.

To this day, Mr. Jones still calls the school, the district office, and the mayor's office. Eventually, I learned that some situations just don't have solutions that "fix it." A principal's job is to try and solve problems. When they can't be fixed, a principal's job also means dealing with frustrations and people who are angry. Was I an ineffective leader because I could not make Mr. Jones happy (and therefore relieve my community of his complaints)? No. Did I feel like an ineffective leader? You bet. Ultimately I learned to own only what is in my sphere of control and to let the rest go.

Principals are held accountable by everyone to fix everything, even if they can't.

The principalship is unique from leadership positions in other organizations because principals are inevitably on point, all the time, for all public relations issues that encompass the entire educational delivery system in America. It would not be uncommon for a principal to be quizzed on his or her stance on federal legislation and how it will ultimately affect the school community while wiping the cafeteria tables after breakfast. It is also just as likely for a mother to stop a principal in the parking lot of a grocery store on a Saturday morning and ask for advice about what is the best kind of educational toy to buy as a birthday gift for a kindergartner. Furthermore, a principal may be required by the crossing guard to defend his view of the best way to punish a child for lying. This wide range of questions comes to the principal from every segment of the community because the principalship is a role that immediately confers omniscience to the person designated as the leader of the school.

Principals are part oracle, part spin-doctor, and part public relations guru for the districts they serve. That is why the selection of a new principal is a somewhat risky business for superintendents. When the selection pools of candidates are limited and/or filled with applicants who are unknown quantities, superintendents and governing boards of education take real gambles by hiring people that they may not know as well as people currently employed in their system. If you were to ask ten randomly selected school superintendents across the country to explain the process used in their district to hire principals, you would undoubtedly hear something like this:

> We in the XYZ School district believe in the importance of hiring the best administrators possible to lead our schools through the new millennium. We conduct national searches for candidates to fill our principalship positions. All qualified applicants are put through several days of intense

screening exercises along with interviews conducted by large committees in an effort to find the person that is the best fit for our school and community.

The depth and scope of these hiring procedures is impressive. In terms of public relations, all this hoop jumping assures that the district is making every effort to find the best leader possible. The rigor of the selection process legitimizes the greatness of the candidate who is ultimately crowned as leader. The reality supporting such a hiring model is rooted in the fact that school principals are asked to become leaders in situations of extraordinary ambiguity. A savvy superintendent realizes that once hired, principals are difficult to influence or control. Superintendents want and need frontline administrators to run their schools that *think like they do*. Additionally, they know that the public firing of a principal is a rare and ugly thing. Thus, an extensive preselection process allows superintendents and governing boards of education some insurance with the new administrator in which they are making an investment.

Unless he or she was a plugged-in insider, the principal may have no clue as to why he or she was chosen. If a new principal were to actually ask a superintendent, "Why did you hire me?" a common answer would be, "You were the best fit." But what does that mean?

Do universities require classes in "how to fit" for their aspiring principals? No. When the personnel director explains that, "You were just not the right fit," to candidates who did not get the job, does he or she go into any further detail? No. Ultimately, *fit* is a wonderfully opaque term that means, "You look and act and think like us. Therefore, we are betting that you will continue to look and act and think like us, even though there is very little we can do to assure your compliance."

The concept of fit is directly related to another word used all the time in the world of leadership: Mission. Everyone knows how to throw the word "mission" around. Most newly hired principals have no sense of what their mission is, in spite of the stellar answers about their dedication to mission given during the interview process. Why is this? Because, generally, principals do not know specifically what their governing boards or superintendents want—except for them to avoid controversy.

FIGURE OUT WHY YOU FIT

What should the principal do who is setting up shop in his or her new office? Ask the superintendent to specifically explain what he or she wants. Start with the question of "What is my mission?" but understand that the question elicits a Pavlovian and oblique response from all administrators. Follow up the mission question with detailed queries in plain language that address what and where you and the superintendent think the path of your school should be under your leadership.

Another strategy that will help you to figure out the new landscape is to ask folks to explain why you fit. Don't limit the question to the superintendent. Ask folks who participated in the hiring process. Talk to a crosssection of people representing all levels of the district so you can see patterns of responses that reflect what the district perceives are your strengths and weaknesses. Furthermore, these insights will serve as clues to help you determine what the behavioral expectations are for principals. Do not assume that you have an advantage if you have ascended to your leadership role from an assistant principalship. The culture of the principalship is completely different than the world of assistant principals. New principals are thrust into a murky environment with very few overt signals as to how things are perceived or valued. Often one of the reasons that principals do not stay in a system for more than five years is because how *they looked* in an interview and how they *fit* were two different things. That being said, consider the following strategies when trying to figure out what the school district's unspoken rules are for determining fit.

Identify the Players That Are Principals and Follow Their Cultural Rituals

Who has the superintendent's ear? What do they look like? Do they present themselves in a certain way in terms of dress, social activities, and interests? First impressions mean something. Yes, it is shallow, but true. Don't stop your efforts to make a good impression just because the interview is over. Look around the next time you are called to a district office meeting of all the administrators. Is everyone in a suit? Conversely, if your superintendent takes casual Friday seriously and gives you a denim "I Love the District" shirt, then you need to wear it with your khaki pants when everyone else does. Does everyone in your district wear those little gold-plated lapel pins of kids walking to school? Even if that pin is hideous and ruins your best jacket—wear it. That little pin says more than "I love kids"; it also says, "I fit, and I understand how to look like a principal in this place."

Maybe some of the other principals play golf and you don't. Maybe they play golf with the superintendent once a month, or with a governing board member. If that is true, you had better learn. Shared activities are a way that people within an organization build relationships. This is important because relationship building is the foundation to getting things done. The more comfortable that people feel around you, the more likely that they will help you learn the ropes. For example, if you are not *playing golf*, you certainly would be *talking about golf* during the breaks at governing board meetings. And of course golf discussion usually leads to other conversations about things like budgets and political agendas.

Perhaps you think that golf is too gender specific? Fine, find something else that is a shared value or interest. Maybe it is being a fan of the Pittsburgh Steelers. Maybe it is going to the same place to get your nails done as everyone else in the district office. Or maybe it is shopping at the most wonderful gourmet store in downtown Akron. Interests and hobbies are what serve as icebreakers and help build relationships. Don't forget all practitioners first learned in Principalship 101 that relationships are the key to successful leadership.

Learn What Fit Means in Terms of Conduct in Administrative Arenas

Does the district or superintendent espouse "shared decision making" but in reality promotes a culture in which offering a dissenting opinion results in banishment to the doghouse? In other words, when is it OK to fight a battle to help your school and when is it not? How do other principals who are viewed as "stars" get and keep their power? To ensure legitimacy of your newly crafted definition of fit, look hard at the administrators that appear to be "on the outs" with the system. Think about what they do, or say, or model that is in direct conflict with what fits and take a lesson from their mistakes. Grasping a real sense of fit and purpose will help a new principal immensely. Often those leaders who have trouble in the beginning encounter bumps because their ego does not allow them to see the culture in which they work or they don't have the patience to demonstrate they fit before running their agenda. Remember, understanding the rules and parameters of your district is not based on just believing what people say. Understanding the subtle rules and values is really based on observing what people do in relationship to what they say. In a perfect world, what we say and how we act are the same. In reality, it is often not the case.

Another unique characteristic of the principalship is that those in charge of schools are automatically viewed as the patriarchs and matriarchs of one huge family. We are seen as therapists, confidants, and the person who has all of the answers. What we wear, how we interact with others, and the kind of car we drive are all up for scrutiny. If we look stressed, then there must be something going on to be stressed about.

We must be mindful that there are two types of behaviors we exhibit that set the tone for our school community: frontstage behavior and backstage behavior. We obviously consider our frontstage behavior when doing things like speaking to groups and facilitating meetings. Our backstage behavior is less formal, less controlled, and less in the forefront of our consciousness. Alicia Crowe, a principal in her fifth year, remembers:

> I once had the fortunate opportunity to have a communications expert spend a few days with me on campus. She followed me around and then gave me an analysis of her observations. I was amazed when she told me to walk slower down the hall. Walk slower? What do you mean walk slower? I have exactly one and one half minutes to get to a teacher evaluation. Then I need to be on the playground; after that I might be able to sneak into the bathroom for thirty seconds before my walkie-talkie reminds me that I have an eleven o'clock meeting with a parent and her attorney who wants to sue the district and remove some of my body parts. I walk down those halls with purpose simply because I am on a mission. I am trying to do my job so that the school is running smoothly.
>
> But strolling down the hall was exactly what I needed to do. Some of my staff assumed that because I walked with purpose that meant I was angry. Had I told anyone I was angry? No. Had anyone ever asked if I was

angry? No. Did it matter that my assistant principal walked the same way when she was on a mission? No.

My mistake was that I forgot my frontstage behavior. Whenever I had a break from a task in the office—I would stroll the halls and manage by walking around. I would chat with folks, enjoy the outdoors, or get involved with a project that kids were doing. I was thinking about being there to communicate and connect with people on my campus. When I was problem solving and checking off projects on the day's to-do list, I walked differently. I had a harder look on my face because I was concentrating on my tasks rather than my frontstage behavior. The staff did not differentiate between the two reasons behind my campus walks. Therefore, people misread what was going on because I was not thinking about my frontstage behavior.

I began to train myself to think about the word "stroll" whenever I left my door. I wrote "stroll" on my walkie-talkie and on the back of my office door. In about two months, a teacher remarked that she had overheard in the teachers' lounge that I seemed so much more relaxed: That I was "easing into the job so much better." In my mind nothing had changed. I still have lots of people wanting lots of things all at once, except now I stroll.

I was also careful to stroll even in the administrative offices. Frontstage behavior is especially important there: Rookies often mistake their relationships with their office staff as more intimate simply because of their physical proximity. It is simply not so—secretaries can be the town criers of information, or misinformation, to your community.

Be Mindful of Frontstage and Backstage Behavior

It is important to remember that frontstage behavior should be an automatic expectation for you as the new person, in a new role in a new school. Being aware of how you are perceived is especially important while trying to figure out the culture of your new school. Even if you were a previous member of the staff you now supervise, allow yourself time to observe and absorb the dynamics of how things work at your school and what is important. This caveat is applicable to the entire culture of the school that ranges from Friday staff happy hours to how the teachers' lounge is decorated. Part of why it is so important to put care into how you let your staff and community get to know you is because of the invisible networks of people that you are working among.

You may make an offhand remark about someone or something that will come back to haunt you because you did not realize that the person you are speaking with has a direct and trusting relationship with someone else who may have power over you politically. Or you may offend someone inadvertently whose support you may need in the future to carry an agenda item to fruition with your community. To further explore the idea of frontstage and backstage behavior, consider the concept of the Johari Window (Luft, 1970). This tool for understanding group dynamics and how people behave is often used in the world of counseling. The name, Johari, refers to the originators, Joe Luft and Harry Ingham. Basically the window looks like this:

	Known to Self	Not Known to Self
Known to Others	I. Area of Free Activity (Public Self)	II. Blind Area ("Bad-Breath" Area)
Not Known to Others	III. Avoided or Hidden Area (Private Self)	IV. Area of Unknown Activity

Essentially, the window illustrates that people behave in ways that can be conceptualized in four quadrants to varying degrees. Sometimes we spend more time in one quadrant than another. The amount of time and effort in each quadrant shifts from day to day and moment to moment depending on the dynamics of the group that we are functioning within.

The first quadrant, the Public Self, is the area of frontstage behavior. This is where we are conscious of what we are doing and how we are perceived. This is where we mind our manners. For administrators, the third quadrant, called the Private Self, is where we exhibit backstage behavior. It is also where our hidden political agendas are. The fourth quadrant, the Area of Unknown Activity, is the category that basically says when something happens to us or around us, we do not yet know how we will behave. For example, a principal may announce at a faculty meeting that if a student were to arrive on campus with a loaded shotgun, he or she would be the first person to ensure that the campus is safe for everyone. What does that really mean? Will the principal calmly confront the student and try to remove the weapon? Will the principal run quickly to the nearest office and call the police and then announce a lockdown? Or will the principal nervously ask for help from the first adult he or she sees? No one (including the principal) knows what this leader will do because this scenario may have never happened before. We can hope that our actions would be one way in circumstances that are uncertain; however, we cannot be sure, because the Area of Unknown Activity is the category that looks at how we behave in novel and unpredictable situations.

For rookies as well as astute politicians, it is important to pay particular attention to the second quadrant, known as the Blind Area. The Blind Area is where we engage in behavior whose effects on other people are blind to us. A simple metaphor would be when we fail to brush our teeth after eating a hamburger with onions and not realizing we have bad breath. Everyone near us may know we smell like onions, but they will not tell us. This blind-to-self behavior plays a large part into *fit*. Remember, *fit* is a key to leading. When we fit, it is easier to lead. A good way to see how *fit* and the Johari Window are related is to consider the "Welcome Back to School" speech that Dr. Ken Riccio, a new principal gave to his staff:

> I am so very pleased to be here leading Harrell High School. I want you to know I am energized and excited to be working as your principal. I have really enjoyed walking the halls watching people get ready for classes this fall. My secretary will be setting up individual meetings with each one of you so I can get to know you better. In the meantime though, I do have an open-door policy and if you ever need me, please come by and say hello.

The fifteen-year veteran English teacher reacted to Dr. Riccio's speech this way:

> Great. . . . Here is another arrogant Ph.D. talking about "I, I, I . . . and me, me, me." Wonder if he ever thinks about "we," or "us"? How can we possibly take this guy seriously until he can talk like we are a team? I suppose he thinks the world just rotates around him.

When she heard Dr. Riccio's speech, the biology teacher in her second year at Harrell High School thought:

> Well, it sounds like the guy cares, but I heard in the lounge that he is always late for everything. I have only been in two meetings with him, but he was late for both. And when he came in he just said "I am so sorry. I owe every one of you ten minutes for being late." What is that supposed to do? Make me feel better? It doesn't. It makes me feel like this is just another administrator who says one thing and does another. I don't trust him.

The faculty representative for the teacher's union heard Dr. Riccio's speech and told her husband:

> You know, I think this guy wants to try and I know he is new to the job. But we have been here for a month already and he is always in his office with the door closed. I know he said he has an open-door policy, but he sure does not act like it. I never see him out and about. How is he ever going to figure out what really happens around here if all he does all day is hide in that office?

Will Dr. Riccio ever hear from anyone that he came off a little arrogant or that he has lost credibility with some of his staff because he is always late to meetings? Probably not. Will anyone ever say to him that he needs to be more visible? Maybe. For now, however, all that is happening is that the gossip and judgment mill is cranking up in the teachers' lounge and Dr. Riccio is trying to figure out how to balance back-to-back meetings designed to help put out the fires on campus. He has not figured out how to have his secretary keep him on track by interrupting meetings and telling him that the next meeting is about to start. He has not figured out that using the word "we" instead of "I" makes a very different impression on some people. These blind-to-self behaviors are making fit a little more difficult for Dr. Riccio. The danger here is that by the time Dr. Riccio realizes that he may need to do some damage control in terms of how he is perceived, it may be too late.

The lessons from Dr. Riccio's blunders are simple but very important. Enter a new school by being aware of how many times you say "I" or "me" or "at my old school we did this or that." These inadvertently egocentric messages give your staff the impression that you are expecting them to adjust to you rather than demonstrating that you are learning to understand their culture. Even though you are indeed the leader, a little graciousness goes a long way. The best move any rookie can make in the beginning is to do lots of watching and listening. Try and figure out who holds the informal power, who gets things done, who gossips, and who listens to the gossip. This effort is easier said than done. Do not assume that you will understand the intricacies of your school networks in a month—it will take even a seasoned professional at least a year of serious efforts to grasp the networks of people he or she serves.

Start by listening to people. Listening is an art unto itself that very few people master. Listening requires you to make eye contact with the person speaking to you. It also requires you to stop fidgeting with the papers on your desk or your e-mail. Good listeners acknowledge what is being said by asking thoughtful questions and repeating certain ideas. Good listeners focus. It is possible to listen to someone even if you are walking to another meeting or to bus duty. Good listeners are also keen observers. Hone you observation skills by making mental notes of who sits with whom in faculty meetings and in the lunchroom. Take roll of the cars in the school parking lot. Soon you will be able to know who stays late, who arrives early, and who is friendly with whom. These efforts will help you to craft a sort of schematic map in your head of what the networks are in your school and in your community.

As you are outlining your network map, take the time to build relationships with the people you are getting to know. Relationships come from efforts that are based on integrity and truth. Taking the time to listen and follow up on a promise, no matter how small, is a huge investment in building integrity (and therefore loyalty) with your staff.

> Relationships based on integrity build networks. The smart rookie creates networks both above and below him or her in a system.

PRINCIPALS LIVE IN A COMPETITIVE ARENA

Another surprising difference found in the principalship is that principals exist in a competitive arena rather than the fraternal one found in the assistant principalship. The principalship brings the new, personalized, pressure of analyzing how your school performs in comparison with other schools in the district. In a sense, the community's concern over test scores, campus violence, or any other global issue becomes personal because the community wants to know what *you, the leader,* are going to do to address the problem. They may hear about strategies a sister school implemented and want to know why you aren't approaching a problem in the same way. Your superintendent will have these same sorts of concerns too.

This sense of comparison or competition can vary depending on the philosophy of your superintendent. Some believe that competition is good and increases efforts and achievements of site administrators while some see it as derisive. Try to figure out the degree of competition in your world. Gauge this competition by watching how people respond to agenda discussions at your districtwide leadership team meetings. Watch how your colleagues speak to and about each other. You may soon discover a pattern of those who are always asking for funds or complaining about their school being the forgotten stepchild of the district. Compare that observation with who seems to always have enough resources for projects. Does your district have a culture where everyone makes backroom deals, or are things more aboveboard? Is your superintendent's cabinet consistent with enforcing the rules concerning staffing ratios, funding, and professional development opportunities? Or, are these things given out as rewards to principals and directors in exchange for something else? Observe carefully the principal who seems to have the most pull. Is he or she the senior administrator or an old friend of the superintendent? Maybe this administrator has a friendship with a governing board member. All of these observations are helpful because your job is to do everything possible to bring forth *your vision* at *your school*. That means you have to fight for the limited resources, opportunities, and all the other stuff that the district has to divide up among its schools.

In the process of fighting for your school, you may end up competing against your closest colleague for a resource such as an extra teacher.

When this happens, remember not to take it personally, this is only business. In addition, do not assume that your colleague will be able to differentiate between personal and business issues. Giving loyalty does not automatically mean you will receive the same amount or kind of loyalty in return. A common mistake is the belief that loyalty is automatically offered from superiors while it is fleeting and tenuous with subordinates. Because the principalship is a lonely position, people are tempted to confide in those with whom they work closest. Be careful. Machiavelli is most correct in that when it comes to the choice between being loyal or saving one's own skin, people will save (or even promote) themselves first.

Do not assume loyalty from anyone, even your superintendent.

CHAPTER 1 INSTANT REPLAY: YOU AREN'T IN TRAINING CAMP ANYMORE

1. The principalship is nothing like the assistant principalship.
2. The principalship is a competitive arena because your job description requires you vie for district resources against your principal colleagues.
3. Don't take competition from your colleagues personally as their job, like yours, is to be loyal to their school above all else.
4. Don't expect loyalty from your teachers, your parents, or your superiors.
5. Be mindful of how you are perceived by those around you and pay attention to frontstage and backstage behavior.
6. Build networks that extend through every level of your organization: Pay as much attention to the janitors as you do the superintendent.
7. Understand what *fit* is. Know why you *fit* and be able to identify what other principals do to *fit*.

8. Respect the culture of your school and your district—if they wear little starfish pins, or apple pins, then you need to also.
9. Keep your word; it is the first thing that people will notice about who you are as a leader.
10. Build networks by listening and showing people you value them.

2

LOCKER ROOM

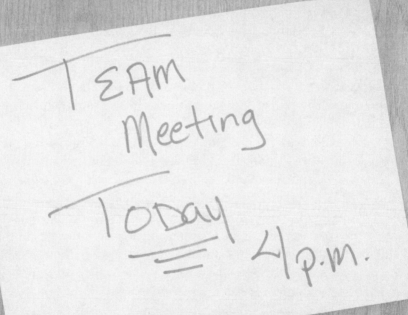

COMMUNICATION
AND THE
TEAM

Mark Estep was riding in the backseat of the car with his wife, Susan. His colleague and fellow curriculum director, Zac Anthony, was driving. Zac's wife, Anna, commented that this evening seemed like the great American double date as the two couples were driving to a Friday night football game at Washington High School. "Honey, why is it so important that we go all the way across town to see Washington's football game?" Anna asked.

Zac replied, "Because I wanted Mark and Susan to see Tiger Town. They have never been to Washington High." Anna whipped around and exclaimed, "You are kidding me! How can you be a school administrator and yet have never seen a Washington football game? You know, no one really *gets football* until they go to Tiger Town."

Mark was tired from a harried day of meetings. He was trying hard to be sociable, but the idea of attending this game after a long day in the trenches was not sounding very good. After all, this was only high school athletics. It is not like they were going to see the Steelers play in Heinz field. And what was Tiger Town anyway? The signs on the road said they were driving to Massillon.

The Massillon neighborhoods boasted lots of houses with signs in the front yards. At first Mark thought they were real estate advertisements; upon closer inspection Mark realized the signs read "Welcome to Tiger Town" or "You are in Tiger Country!" The signs were all over the place. Mark wondered aloud, "Are we close to the school? Is tonight a big game for Washington? There are so many houses with signs in the yard I figured that these folks must have kids who are on the football team." Zac answered back, "Nope, the school is a few miles north of here. We are not in Washington's neighborhood yet. Tonight is not really a big matchup. These houses belong to folks that are just fans. People take their football pretty seriously around here."

Zac was not kidding. When the car finally parked in Washington's stadium lot, Mark was surprised at the number of tailgating revelers he saw, particularly because it was raining. Washington's school colors, orange and black, were everywhere. The sights and sounds of a Friday night football game were nothing new to Mark. However, he could not help but be struck by the sheer number of people attending the game. Coming to Tiger Town was an event; something that families did regardless of whether they had children who went to Washington High School.

Mark was also impressed with the cultural symbols in the Washington community. References to Tiger pride and Tiger values were everywhere. Moreover, Tiger pride was something that extended beyond the realm of football. Gas station windows proclaimed Tiger Students of the Month. The schools administrative offices had showcased pictures of exceptional and creative teachers working in the classroom. There was even a "Washington Wall of Fame" where photographs of community members were displayed.

It wasn't just the signs and photographs that demonstrated to visitors how special Tiger Town was. The people working the football game were equally impressive to visitors. From the principal on the field to the policeman in the stands to the janitor sweeping the sidewalks, everyone accomplished their tasks with ease. All of these things added up to an atmosphere that radiated efficiency, effectiveness, and a community sense of pride.

Mark asked a teacher handing out game programs what made Tiger Town so extraordinary. She replied, "This is just a fun place to be. We really value family here and we want to see our kids succeed." Mark thought about how this young lady sounded like a commercial for the school. He then asked her if she was repeating a mission statement that perhaps she had seen on a wall or bulletin board. She told him:

> No, I don't really know what a mission statement is. What I do know is that I like the people I work with and I trust them. I believe in my principal because he gets things done. This place is pretty organized and I think that has a lot do with how secure it feels. I like knowing pretty much how my day at work will go. It's not that there are a million rules; it's just that all of us here understand how things are supposed to be in our school. From what a good student is to what a good teacher is, to what it takes to make a difference. You know, maybe that is the key for us: Everyone in Tiger Town understands the way things are supposed to be.

COMMUNICATING HOW THINGS ARE SUPPOSED TO BE

The tone of a school's environment is not something that simply happens. It is a palpable result of a principal's communication efforts at every level of his or her school.

The essence of the principalship boils down to two interdependent tasks: (a) figuring out the way things are supposed to be in a school community, and (b) communicating *effectively* how things are supposed to be to all members of a school community. These chores require an understanding of the factions involved in a school system along with the relationship they have to each other and the principal. Consider the layers of constituencies that affect a principal by looking at figure 2.1, called the Web of Constituencies.

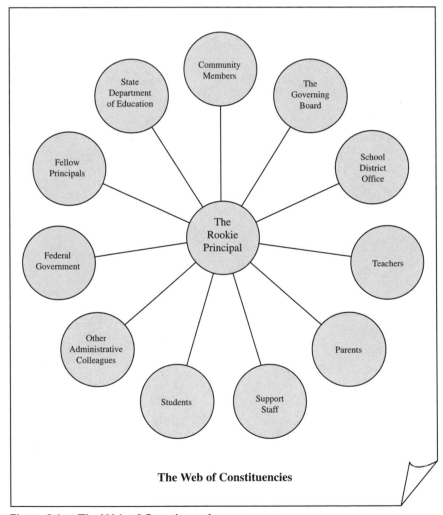

The Web of Constituencies

Figure 2.1.   The Web of Constituencies

Each constituency (identified in a circle) is defined by its own unique agenda, culture, and perspective. The principal is represented in the center of the web because these cohorts are usually in competition with each other for his or her time and support. Because of these tensions, school leaders often find themselves acting as shuttle diplomats and information brokers, working to balance the systemic tension caused by the competition and demands of these constituencies. Because each group is different, the type of effort exerted by the principal to maintain balance varies. This results in principals making regular efforts to triage demands while reviewing their daily schedule.

Holly Seimetz, an assistant principal at The Rayen School, uses her drive to work as the opportunity to think about how she is going to balance the tensions in her school system. This is how she explains the morning drive strategy session to a fellow passenger in her car:

OK. . . . Let's get the calendar flipped open and I'll try not to hit the van in front of me. First thing is substitute coverage, checking on who called in sick and if there is a substitute to cover class. If there is not a substitute available, I need to figure out which teachers can cover on their prep periods. I can do that on the phone while I am driving. After the secretaries and I solve those problems, I am usually halfway to the school building. Once I get to school I go straight to bus duty. There are thirteen buses that arrive between 7:30 and 7:45 every morning. Usually there are one or two fights and several reports of disrespectful behavior toward the bus driver. After I process all those discipline referrals, I am scheduled to observe and evaluate two teachers before ten o'clock. I have a district meeting at 10:30 to go over the new school district mandates to prove to the federal government that our school is in compliance with the No Child Left Behind Act. If I can slip out of the meeting half an hour early, I'll be able to make the three o'clock CPR meeting for all coaches at a neighboring school. I have a student expulsion hearing scheduled at 4:30 with the superintendent, so I can't be late to that. I promised I would go to our school's birthday club at 6:30, so I could celebrate my principal's birthday. In between the district office where the expulsion hearing is held and the restaurant where Birthday Club is meeting, there is a card store. I can pick up my principal's card and a little present on the way to the club meeting. I'll be a little late, but I can blame it on the hearing and beg forgiveness. Even though Birthday Club is at 6:30 and the district governing board meeting starts at 7:00, I can be late to the board meeting because I am not speaking. I just need to sit in the audience and be seen. I can catch up paperwork for the homecoming assembly and organize the roster of teachers who are giving extra help to students who failed their standardized proficiency tests while I am sitting at the board meeting tonight. After the board meeting, the Women in Leadership Society is getting together at the Springfield Grille. This book club was formed by our assistant superintendent. It is for female administrators to think and talk with each other about issues in leadership. Attendance is not mandatory, but I think it is good politics to show up. I didn't have time to read the book for tonight's discussion, but maybe I can fake it. Besides, I heard that one of the guests speaking is a principal from Cleveland. This lady's leadership team brought her school's test scores up 123 percent last year, and I want to hear how she did that. After that meeting I am hoping to grab a cup of coffee with Donald Kennedy. Donald is the assistant principal at our sister school and it would be nice to check in with him and see how he is handling a few of our teachers who transferred over to his school last summer. Besides, investing in a professional relationship with Donald is smart because when April rolls around this year, I will have to ask him for help organizing the districtwide Olympics.

What Holly is doing within this monologue is deciding how much time and effort to give each constituent that she is involved with on this particular day. Massaging schedules, taking advantage of professional growth opportunities, making political investments, and building relationships are what frame her decisions concerning how she spends her day. The savvy principal realizes that effective communication is dependent on the ability of the communicator to understand his or her audience. Understanding your audience happens only when you have built some kind of relationship with them. And relationships start with face time and listening.

If this axiom sounds trite to you, think again. Listening is the most important skill in the effective administrator's repertoire. Listening carefully and with purpose allows the school principal to build an understanding of the infrastructure and network of constituencies in a school community.

THE DIRT ON LISTENING

Listening is commonly defined as the practice of making a conscious effort to hear or to pay attention closely. In terms of leadership, the definition should be expanded to include the concept that listening is one of simplest and yet most important acts a person can perform to validate another. One of the common complaints teachers have concerning school leaders is that, "The principal just doesn't listen." Why is that?

The primary answer to this question refers back to figure 2.1, the Web of Constituencies. Principals are required to switch mental gears several hundred times a day because of all the situations, problems, and people that they encounter. This gear switching gets in the way of listening, particularly when one also has to multitask.

Principals, like other politicians, are approached by folks with concerns while they are "on their way" somewhere. Most problems or agendas come to the principal's attention in the halls of a school. Agendas that are presented in meetings do indeed allow time for a principal to focus. Unfortunately a principal may have trouble listening because he or she has participated in so many meetings on a particular day that he or she is just tired. And when you are tired or thinking about how to deal with the problems presented in the previous meeting, it is hard to listen to what is going on in the current meeting. That being said, some ideas on how to listen effectively are presented below:

Listening Tricks

- Look people in the eye when they are talking to you; maintain eye contact with them while they are speaking.
- If you are in the hallway or a group, and someone is speaking to you, fight the temptation to interrupt that person in favor of switching your attention to another person nearby.
- Repeat back occasionally what you are hearing in your own words by saying, "What I am hearing you say is ..."
- If a person is angry or ranting and raving, let them. Be quiet and maintain eye contact. When they stop, ask politely, "What is it you need from me?" Sometimes all they needed was for you to listen. Often the person will realize that there is nothing you can do other than to listen.
- Take some notes on the details the person is telling, but do not go overboard and leave people believing you are more concerned with note-taking than listening.
- If you find it hard to concentrate while someone is talking, drink a glass of water or shift positions in your chair.

Timing is another factor related to communication. Information, like cold remedy capsules, is time released through an organizational system. For example, when the principal hears he has to completely change his reading program, he knows that to some degree he must strategize when to break the news to the teachers. Tell them too early without details and the teachers will be up in arms about change and the lack of planning. Tell the teachers too late and the information may have already leaked through the organizational structures. A succession of these types of blunders can lead to morale problems and the perception that the principal is unorganized.

To understand how information moves through a system, one must give consideration to how information ripples from the principal to his or her staff. On the most basic level one assumes that information trickles through the lines of rank, from principal to assistant to teacher to aide, and so on. These ripples can be categorized as both purposeful and inadvertent planes. Examples of information that is purposefully communicated through a system are memos in teachers' boxes, classroom teaching observation reports, or letters home to parents. However, information can inadvertently move through the system via groups of people that have positional proximity to the principal. To better understand this dynamic, consider figure 2.2, Proximity Levels and Information Flow. Principals have the most contact on a communication level with office staff. This is because it is usually the staff's job to help the principal organize and distribute all the types of communication related to the principalship. Levels radiating out from the office staff increase in the actual number of people but decrease in the amount of actual time spent with the principal.

A common illustration of how the principal can intend to move purposeful information through a system, only to discover that it has inadvertently rippled through his school, is the following story about Trent Hess. Trent is the new assistant principal at Allison High School. He has been charged with the responsibility of evaluating the teaching skills of a special education teacher named Kim Sargent. After several classroom observations, Trent decides that Mrs. Sargent needs to be on a plan of improvement. As Trent begins to write up the plan on his computer, he asks his secretary to come into his office to order some more athletic equipment for the PE department. The secretary, who is on the same

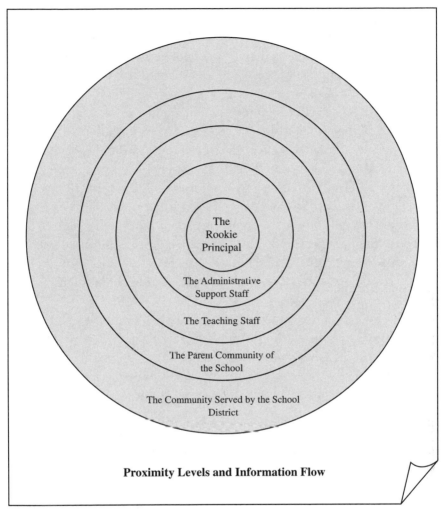

The
Rookie
Principal

The Administrative
Support Staff

The Teaching Staff

The Parent Community of
the School

The Community Served by the School
District

Proximity Levels and Information Flow

Figure 2.2. Proximity Levels and Information Flow

bowling team as Kim's sister Alice, notices what is written on his computer.

Nine hours later at the Milford bowling lanes, the secretary hints in ambiguous terms to Alice that Kim should watch out for the new administrator. The secretary avoids details because she believes that if she divulges any more information that it would be unprofessional. Alice calls Kim on the way home from bowling to gossip. And the next morning, Trent gets a call from Mary Doyle, the district's teachers' union representative. Mrs.

Doyle wants to discuss Kim Sargent's unfair teaching evaluation. Trent is taken by surprise because he has not even finished writing the evaluation. What has happened here is that Trent is not aware of the subtle nuances of the networks of people with whom he works. Why? Because he is new. Also, he was not thinking about who would see what on his computer. He was simply trying to get his job done as efficiently as possible. Trent's secretary doesn't believe that she did anything wrong because she had heard in the lounge that Kim was having a bad year because her husband left her. By telling Alice, the secretary thought she was helping Kim to save her job. Furthermore, Trent is the new guy and no one really trusts him yet. The problem now is that Kim Sargent feels angry and resentful about an evaluation she has not even seen. Trent has to deal with the backlash of being viewed as the new guy who is out to get someone. This problem could have been avoided if Trent had understood that the information can ripple (or leak) through a system not only through lines of rank but also through the lines of physical proximity.

Communication through the lines of proximity are related to a principal's efforts to balance the demands of varying constituencies. Therefore, the Web of Constituencies (figure 2.1) and Proximity Levels and Information Flow (figure 2.2) actually exist in tandem, forming a Communication Matrix in which principals exist (figure 2.3).

For principals, working in the matrix means that every effort made to meet systemic tensions can be overheard or misinterpreted by anyone in the organization at any time. Thus, misinterpretations of information can ripple through the system, forcing the principal to stop what project he or she is currently focused on in order to put out political fires. Some principals never learn to influence the flow of information in their organizations, so they spend a lot of time putting out fires. Others learn the subtleties of these networks and use them to help move an agenda forward.

WHAT TO DO WITH A COMMUNICATION FUMBLE

If you find yourself in a place where the ripples of information have become tsunamis, deal with the fallout by first triaging who knows what. Assess how this situation affects your political agenda, your power, and

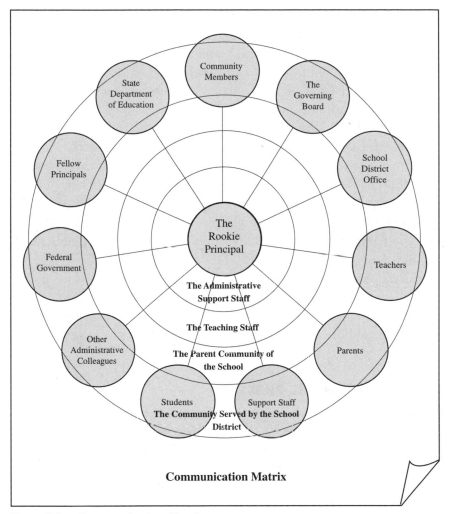

Figure 2.3. Communication Matrix

your credibility with your constituencies. If necessary, seek the aid of a trusted colleague to help brainstorm a strategy to resolve the situation. Before you take any action in terms of talking to the people involved, take the time to free yourself from any ego or emotional attachment. Many principals have made a bad situation worse because they let their temper, anxieties, or ego get in the way of effectively controlling a mess.

Another important strategy is to become cognizant of *spin*. Spin is the word used to describe the art of reframing information to fulfill a particular agenda. Spinning information is not the same as lying; it is merely a tool that effective leaders use to change how people see an issue. A very simple example of spin would be the football coach who explains to his wife that he is not overweight, he is simply underheight.

Redefining the problem, as the football coach did, is a preferred tactic for many school administrators. For instance, when the superintendent of an Arizona school district was confronted with a barrage of criticism because his district had one of the lowest graduation rates in the state, he deftly responded by stating that the problem wasn't the graduation rate, but rather the student retention rate. He then focused all of his efforts toward increasing the ways in which teachers recorded the average daily attendance and average daily membership of his school. He instilled reward systems to ensure that teachers and support staff were accurately recoding attendance. He also encouraged his administrative staff to create incentives for students to stay in school. After two years, the student attrition rate decreased. Was there a change in the proficiency exam scores? No. Was the superintendent hailed as a great leader? Yes, because the community and the press agreed that he "got kids to stay in school."

DEALING WITH THE PRESS

Many school districts have on staff a public information officer, or PIO. A PIO is someone who does many things, but their most important function is to deal with the press. Districts who do not use a PIO usually assign public relations responsibilities to the superintendent or assistant superintendent. Make a point to meet with whomever tackles public relations issues and to ask for mentorship concerning how your district wants administrators to deal with issues concerning the press. In addition to the insights offered by your media point person, refer to the checklist in figure 2.4 for pointers.

CREATING AND MANAGING COMMUNICATIONS SYSTEMS

The odds are that when you join an administrative staff, there will be several communications systems in place. Do not assume, however, that

Media Relations

- You may need to speak to a reporter after working an 18 or 20 hour day (particularly after a school emergency). Be prepared by keeping a fresh, clean white shirt and a dark jacket hanging on the back of your office door at all times. If you need to be interviewed, remember that television photographers shoot from the waist up. A fresh shirt and jacket make you look more rested and a dark jacket shows up the best on camera.

- Keep deodorant, toothbrush, eye drops, and other grooming items on hand (including a clean necktie and/or a new pair of pantyhose). Before going on camera, clean up a little. The five minutes it takes to refresh yourself is also time to shift gears from the chaos that is happening at your campus to thinking about what you are going to say to the reporter and how you are going to say it.

- Give your superintendent a heads-up that you are being interviewed by a television crew. Before the interviews, he or she may want to talk to you about how to frame your answers. Pay attention to what news station and the name of the reporter. Ask what time the piece will be aired and have someone at your school or district tape the interview for you, so that later you can go back and review your performance.

- Avoid using the word "I" during the interview, as it conveys arrogance to the listener. You are not the king or queen of your school; you are a member of a team. Choose phrasing such as "our team" or "we," or "our school community."

- The art of interviewing lies in giving one clear sound bite over and over, regardless of the question. Give your statement of what happened to the reporter and then avoid details if you are not ready to divulge specific information. End with a statement that is meant to reassure the listener that your campus is safe. For example, "A small weapon was found today in our north campus men's rest room. We are currently in the midst of investigating the students that might be involved. All of our staff is committed to ensuring that this campus continues to be a safe and orderly environment for our students."

- Reporters will try and probe you through questions for more salacious information that could be taken out of context in the editing room. Anticipate these kinds of questions before meeting with the reporter (a good time to do this is when you are taking that five minutes to put on that fresh shirt and dark jacket). When they are asked, answer with the same sound bite that you had created before. Do not let a reporter catch you off guard. To see this technique in action watch any press briefing on CNN or another news station.

- Practice answering questions with another colleague before you have to actually deal with the press.

- Explain to your staff that if a reporter stops them they are to defer any questions to you. You do not need to risk PR gaffs by teachers who are not trained in media relations.

Figure 2.4.   Media Relations Checklist

these systems are effective or efficient. To assess these systems, get a large twelve-month calendar that allows lots of space for notes on every date. Then collect all the printed schedules you can find related to your school. Organize the schedules into three groups: *Information to Parents, Information to Staff,* and *Information to the District Office.* The

Information to Parents category should have things like the athletic events schedule, the report card schedule, the school calendar, and parent organization meetings schedule. The Information to Staff category should include things like the master schedule, teacher professional development dates, and committee meeting dates. The Information to the District Office category should contain any items that have to do with district-centered activities such as districtwide meetings for administrators, CPR certification meetings for coaches, governing board meeting dates, and the due dates of specific reports, such as quarterly discipline summaries.

Take your blank twelve-month calendar and fill in all the dates mentioned on all the calendars you collected. The master calendar you are creating will give you a view into the matrix of communication at your school. Next, look for glitches in the matrix by starting with the parent group of schedules. Find the date that parents can expect to see their child's report card. Now start thinking backward and look at the staff schedule. Ask yourself these questions: Does the staff know when their student progress reports are due to the administrative offices? Does the staff know when grade deficiency reports are due? Look on the master calendar to see if you have notated when the staff should be reminded to turn in the reports.

Analyzing calendars is a two-step process. The first step focuses on how different schedules for all the constituencies in a school system mesh. For example, when looking to see if all the schedules mesh, ask yourself if the teachers as well as the parents know when the winter choir concert is. Is there a reminder on your personal calendar so that you do not miss the concert? Do you know when the unity club is having their bake sale? Is there a system in place to assure that not only the staff knows about club events but that you do as well? The second step of analyzing your school's calendars is the process of following the stream of communication to see if it is complete through all levels of a school community. For instance, look at another category, proficiency tests. Do parents know when the proficiency tests are? Are there dates that tell the teachers to start preparing their students for the proficiency exams? What dates have you noted in the master calendar to in-service the teaching staff about the proficiency scores from the previous year? When are you going to strategize with the staff the changes necessary for students to have more support for the upcoming tests? Is there also a date that outlines when a presentation has to be made to the governing board about how your students performed on these tests?

All of these efforts will eventually lead you to a master calendar that should outline events that occur every school year and the communication necessary to the stream of people involved with them. You can create a reminder file of sorts by translating all the activities for each month into a series of reminders for you, the administrator. Give yourself some added support by occasionally asking the staff for input. Ask them when they really count on reminders from the office. Better yet, ask them to share with you war stories of when there were times that the office forgot to complete a task on the yearly file and how it affected them. A good example here would be ordering supplies. Usually offices are asked to complete supply orders for the fall semester by June. If supplies are not ordered when August rolls around, the teachers who are organizing their classrooms can feel a sense of panic because the supplies they needed are not available.

As you go through the months on the master calendar, add in the reminders that you need to take care of to ensure a smooth opening and closing of school. Note when you want to have your annual letter to parents written. Most administrators send a letter home once a month. Do you have a weekly newsletter for staff? Have you plotted out on your calendar when you are going to visit classrooms and conduct teaching observations and evaluations? The reason why most administrators get into trouble concerning evaluations is because they failed to follow correct timelines. Avoid this rookie mistake by plugging them in your calendar.

SCHEDULING POSITIVE REINFORCEMENT

A powerful secret weapon that effective principals use is the consistent positive reinforcement or praise of their staff. Recognizing the good work that people do helps build morale and loyalty in any organization. However, this seemingly easy task becomes somewhat of an afterthought for the constantly stressed and busy administrator. While it is easiest to pass a compliment on verbally, investing the time in a short note of thanks can make a huge difference in the tone of your school's environment. Recognize people for not only doing a good job but for the actions they take that demonstrate to you that they are supporting your agenda.

Adults, like children, appreciate those small tangible things that recognize their efforts. If you do not agree with this view, make a note of how many cards or notes you see sitting on your teachers' desks while you are touring the campus. The most efficient way to stay on top of this task is to schedule days in your personal calendar every month in which you write short but sincere notes of appreciation to staff. You don't have to write the entire staff in one day. But you can keep a tally of who you recognize in your personal planner and decide that you will recognize five teachers every Friday. A very reasonable goal is to set up a system in which every person who works on your campus gets two notes from you a year. Get your staff roster and plug in the names of people to recognize in groups of five every week. That way, when you attend the governing board meeting and are sitting in the audience, you can open your planner to find five cards and the names of five people to give kudos to. Take care to be consistent in this task. If you start out with the intentions to send notes to everyone and then forget, you earn the reputation of playing favorites. In the end, the efforts necessary to help all in your school family understand how things work boils down to purposefully moving your agenda through the communication networks with consistency and integrity.

CHAPTER 2 INSTANT REPLAY: BEING AN EFFECTIVE COMMUNICATOR

1. The savvy principal also uses words, symbols, rituals, and modeling to help people understand how things are supposed to be in their school.
2. The principal exists in a multidimensional matrix of constituencies; each one requires different sorts of efforts to meet its needs.
3. Information can leak through a system unintentionally; effective principals make efforts to keep this from happening.
4. If there is a communication fumble, analyze the political fallout and act accordingly to resolve the situation.

5. Do not take action when you are angry—you lose your edge and may say or do something you will regret later.

6. Keep a stash of media-ready supplies for when the press knocks on your door.

7. Strategize with a superior ahead of time as to how you are expected to handle the media.

8. Learn how to really listen to the people with whom you work.

9. Invest in organizing a yearlong reminder file to understand how communication flows through your system.

10. Consistent personal notes of recognition are one of smartest investments you can make in helping people to understand and follow your expectations.

3

THE XS AND OS OF TEACHING

The teacher-recruiting fair at Arizona State University was a zoo. Six thousand sweaty educators were crammed into every space available inside the campus activity center. While some of these folks were principals and personnel directors hoping to find quality last-minute hires, the majority of those strutting around in professional dress were newly minted College of Education graduates hungry for a teaching job. Rounding out this annual cattle-call event was a contingent of veteran teachers scouting more attractive positions.

The environment was dense with cologne, resumes, and the anxiety of people wanting to confirm their future for the upcoming school year. Karen Murphy, the longtime principal of Stout High School, mumbled, "I need a break from these insipid fifteen-minute interviews." She excused herself from the makeshift Meet and Greet area her district had set up and walked toward the balcony for some air. To her surprise, Karen found one of her previous students standing near the door wearing a newly pressed blue suit. "Hi, Mrs. Murphy! How are you?!"

"Samantha? Samantha Anthony? Is that you? Why I haven't seen you in years. You look so professional in that suit. How are you? Are you looking for a teaching position?" Samantha smiled and politely said, "Actually, I am looking for several. I am the new principal at Jackson Middle School. I have to find an art teacher, two special ed teachers, and PE coach."

Karen almost fell over. "Oh, God, am I getting old. I am so sorry. . . . I thought you were a new *teacher*. I am so embarrassed. I still think of you as my favorite volleyball player. Remember when we beat Perry in the state finals? You were great in that game. I can't believe you are all grown up and running a school. How are your interviews going? Any prospects?"

Samantha smiled and said," Well to be honest, Mrs. Murphy, this is a little more difficult than I thought it would be. I had twenty interviews this morning and all of the people were OK. But no one really jumped out at me and I am not sure I want just an 'OK' teacher. I want the best at my school, but it looks like this is all I have to choose from. The students arrive in two weeks and I think I am running out of options in terms of where to look for qualified applicants. I thought I knew what a great teacher looked and acted like, but now I am confused. I am not sure that I can pick the next great thing from a pool of applicants. And what happens once I hire them? I mean, I was a PE teacher and now I am supposed to evaluate reading teachers. I know what a good PE lesson looks like, but how can I have any credibility with my staff with no training in the subjects they teach? What if I screw up and keep weak teachers because I am not sure what I am looking at in the classroom? Oh great, there's my human resources guy calling me back to our table. . . . Listen, here is my card, let me know if we can have coffee or something. I would love your advice and it would be fun to catch up. It was great to see you!"

With that, Samantha walked away, leaving her old principal to think about the questions she had asked. Karen told herself that she would indeed have coffee with her newest colleague. She decided the most important insight to share with Samantha would be that the questions she was wrestling with were not exclusive to rookies. Scouting good talent, training raw talent, and supporting teachers to give their professional best is what most principals spend their entire career trying to master.

SCOUTING THE NEXT "BEST THING"

The worst time of year for principals is the end of summer. That is when the need to hire the very best teacher available is met head-on by the pressure to find anyone qualified to fill the empty slots on the master schedule. This confluence of diametrically opposed interests can obscure a principal's standards where teacher candidates are concerned. The first thing to do to protect yourself from this maddening perspective is to decide earlier in the school year (preferably at a moment when you are relaxed) what you think a good teacher is. Use the questionnaire in figure 3.1 to help you define the concept of good teaching.

After completing the good teacher questionnaire, answer these questions again, only substitute the word *excellent* for *good*. When considering each question, look at what you answered for a good teacher and think about how your definitions could be raised to the next level. When you have completed this second set of answers, you now have a working definition of an excellent teacher.

Good teachers can talk to me about their subject matter or grade taught in the following ways:
  1_____
  2_____
  3_____

Good teachers demonstrate to me that they are passionate about their job by doing these things:
  1_____
  2_____
  3_____

Good teachers say the following things about classroom management:
  1_____
  2_____
  3_____

I like these qualities in a good teacher:
  1_____
  2_____
  3_____

I can't stand these qualities and they are non- negotiable, no matter how good the teacher:
  1_____
  2_____
  3_____

These are the strengths that I personally have that I want to see reflected in the behavior of the teachers that I hire:
  1_____
  2_____
  3_____

Good teachers demonstrate that they are good colleagues by doing and saying these things:
  1_____
  2_____
  3_____

Figure 3.1.   The Good Teacher Questionnaire

Finally, do the reverse: Replace the word *good* with the word *acceptable*. Look at the answers you gave for good teaching and adjust your framework down a notch to reveal the minimum standards a teacher can demonstrate that you are willing to work with. When you have completed all three questionnaires, you will see a spectrum of answers that illustrates your values about teaching and learning. Save this information for your own reference at different times of the year. When hiring season comes, refer to these lists again to help you make the best possible hiring choices.

Susan, a principal in her fifth year, explains how she used this approach:

After I filled out the Good, Excellent, and Acceptable questionnaires, I started thinking about what I saw in terms of patterns in my answers. I noticed that the word loyalty was on every single sheet. What seemed to me to shift from each level was an understanding of curriculum. In other words, I learned that I believe excellent teachers know their subject matter inside and out. They make efforts to continue to grow in their knowledge about their subjects and they are open to new ideas. Good teachers have command of their subject matter but don't necessarily make efforts to continue to grow. And for me, acceptable teachers know a little of their subject matter but are at least willing to improve. Where loyalty is concerned, I learned that I have no tolerance for a teacher who may deliver instruction exceptionally well but is not a team player and loyal to his or her colleagues or his or her school community.

I also thought about classroom management and how that relates to the context of instructional delivery. For example, last summer I knew going into the August teacher recruiting fair that I needed an art teacher who was passionate about art, who was creative in what he or she did, and who loved kids. I met a young man who was indeed an artist first and a teacher second. He was pretty laid back in the interview, especially when we talked about student discipline. But when he got to talking about the things he had created with kids, he turned into this ball of fire. He got so worked up about the things his kids contributed to his school. I interviewed another art teacher who was real big on classroom discipline, but not as passionate about creating things and building a community art program. I decided to hire the first guy. Because he was so ambiguous in his interview answers about classroom management, I anticipated that he might have a few problems; but I was willing to invest in him. When I hired him, I shared my reservations concerning his classroom management skills. When school started I had some complaints from other teachers that the kids were running wild in his classroom. My classroom visits proved to me that, indeed, he ran a loose ship. I really kept tabs on him all semester. It seemed that I was in his class at least once a week. And you know, by the end of the year

I not only had a creative teacher who gave lots to our community through art shows and sculpture fairs, I had a competent classroom manager as well. Investing in him took a chunk of my time and I ended up ignoring another teacher who needed some direction to be stronger in curriculum. However, I don't regret it, because I value art as a way to build school culture and community pride. I know the trade-off is that next year, I'll just have to focus on the other teacher.

For most principals it isn't just one other teacher who needs extra attention, it is four, five, or ten. Therein lies the difficulty of being the curriculum leader of a school: finding the balance between investing in teachers to help them improve, praising the ones on top of their game, and working to get rid of those who are beyond help.

A great part of knowing what a good teacher is comes from being out and about on your campus. Seeing teachers *teach* will help you to decide what you admire and respect in the classroom and what you don't. Educating yourself in various areas of curriculum will also help. Young principals often wonder how one is supposed to become a curriculum expert and a leader simultaneously. Mastering these two parallel tasks requires time and patience. Do not expect to become a curriculum guru in one year. The rookie year is about socializing to the position by watching, listening, and thinking about how things work, not only in terms of politics as explained before, but also in terms of how students learn and how teachers function in the classroom. Consider a rookie year to be a success if by June, the school is still relatively calm and you are still excited and happy to be the principal.

In order to survive, successful principals allow themselves breathing room. However, they don't wallow in the notion that because the learning curve of administration is so steep, it is acceptable to remain ignorant about the art of teaching and the science of curriculum. Because principals can't build a deep knowledge base of curriculum in all areas, what happens is that a leader chooses to explore one or two areas in depth because of his or her personal interest.

Or, principals might eschew curriculum areas altogether, with the belief that they should empower their instructional specialists to be the experts. Beware of this philosophy. Empowering your support staff is one matter: Losing credibility as the instructional leader because you don't have enough time or interest to be conversant in curriculum areas is another thing entirely. Too many schools suffer with this dysfunctional dynamic: The principal visits class, watches a lesson for fifteen minutes, and writes up a positive evaluation for the teacher because the students were on task and there were no discipline problems.

At the same time, the instructional specialist sees the same teacher and has great concerns because while the students are having a good time in class, there is not an authentic assessment of learning. The instructional specialist feels intimidated to tell the principal in blunt terms that he or she is not seeing warning signs in the classroom because of the principal's positional power.

Wise school administrators empower their instructional leaders by having the self-discipline to visit teachers and ask them what they are doing. These leaders attend and participate in the district-level curriculum meetings to discuss new instructional programs. Furthermore, effective leaders stay current by subscribing and *reading* professional journals such as *Kappan, Educational Leadership*, and *The Reading Teacher* that focus on teaching and leadership.

To lead, one must model a willingness to shift from teacher to learner and to openly reflect on what each experience means. Consider hosting book talks with your staff about issues that are central to the instructional challenges (see the Principal as Reader section in chapter 11 for ideas on what to read and how to facilitate a book talk). Use your classroom visits and the advice of trusted colleagues to determine the stellar teachers on campus. And reflect on what you see in your classroom visits that matches what is written on the good teaching questionnaire (figure 3.1). Ask teachers you respect what *they think* are difficult issues about a text or program they are using.

When a teacher comes to you with a concern about an instructional issue, listen carefully, and if you think his or her view is legitimate, pass it on to those folks who should know at the district office. Invest the time to follow up with teachers about what you did to help their views be heard throughout the district. These efforts enhance your credibility and build loyalty. The greatest initial investment of time you can make is to set aside in your calendar, every year, four days in which you teach a class—all day. Mark on your calendar, each semester, one day that you teach subjects you are comfortable with and one day that you stretch yourself and teach a subject out of your repertoire. If you were a high school PE teacher—great—take over a PE class. If you were a science teacher—teach science. This approach allows you to demonstrate your expertise by teaching what you are comfortable with as well as a willingness to grow professionally by stretching into a subject out of your area. Use these guest-teaching days as public relations opportunities with your staff by rewarding a teacher for a good deed. Or have a random drawing at a faculty meeting to see who gets the day out of class. Do not be intimidated to teach a class outside the subject area that you were initially trained to teach. A principal who teaches demonstrates willingness to model professional growth to his or her staff. Ask the teacher for whom you are substituting to collaborate with you in construction of a lesson plan that is aligned to what is currently happening in class. Collaborating on a lesson plan gives you a chance to see how any particular teacher thinks about instructional delivery. The bottom line is that your own personal belief of what constitutes a good teacher is something that comes from your own experiences in the classroom as a practitioner, as well as an administrator. Like physicians, educators need to mindfully keep their teaching skills sharp. Furthermore, the definition of school leadership includes a person's willingness to model this commitment.

SETTING EXPECTATIONS

The key to strong, effective leadership rests in the ability to articulate your own beliefs about what, specifically, is "good" teaching. Efforts to consistently communicate these beliefs come in many forms. These range from modeling good teaching to hosting book talks about educational issues, to giving consistent quality feedback within the evaluation process. The aforementioned practices are particularly important at the beginning of a principal's tenure. The first year of a principalship is one of watching and learning for the principal and staff. How you choose to project yourself, your values, and your expectations will affect the tone and culture for the next several years of your administration.

A helpful way to remain mindful of your expectations concerning the classroom on a daily basis is to distill the answers you gave on the Good, Excellent, and Acceptable questionnaires into three or four beliefs that you keep with you at all times. Make these values the mantra you project to your constituencies. Have them written on your clipboard or in your day planner. Turn them into a slogan that is on the top of your letterhead. Or, take a cue from corporate practice and paint them above the doorway in your office. That way, every time you leave your office you will read them, and so will everyone else who leaves your office. Your expectations should also appear in the faculty and community newsletters, as well as in the feedback you give teachers.

For example, if one of your mantra statements is that all students will be treated with dignity in your school, include that statement in the goals section of your teacher evaluations. If your teacher does a great job of classroom management, reinforce your expectations by writing on the evaluation instrument, "Continue to honor students' dignity through your disciplinary procedures." If a teacher has some room to grow in terms of student discipline write, "Challenge yourself to focus on maintaining and enhancing student dignity through classroom procedures." Almost any value or expectation can be expressed through the feedback formula of "Continue to . . ." or "Focus on . . ."

What you expect should be so clear, and easy to understand, that when people talk about you in your absence, your views concerning teaching are mentioned in the same way that aspects of your personality are mentioned. Your pedagogical philosophy should be something that is seen as an innate and intimate part of who you are, much like hair color or fashion sense.

Entire leadership books are dedicated to the art of setting expectations within an organization. Yet the one problem leadership gurus often ignore is the difficulty of maintaining consistency in a chaotic system. Put simply, this author realizes that a new principal is reading the previous passages of this book thinking to himself or herself, "Yeah, all this sounds good, but there is not enough time for me to teach all day. There is no way I can do that. I spend most of my day dealing with angry parents and cranky teachers and suspending kids. The last thing on my mind is getting away from all the fires to teach. Teaching would be a great luxury but I simply can't afford it. I have to run the school." Are you thinking this? Well STOP. Take a breath, and listen to Donald Kennedy's story:

I have been a principal now for fifteen years. I have served as the cur-riculum leader and commander in chief for a high school, and a middle school. Both were full of at-risk kids and in the middle of transition. When I started at Mountain High I felt completely overwhelmed with just the flow of the day. It seemed like every day was a blizzard. I would come into work at six in the morning to answer e-mails, write memos, and complete reports in peace. Before I could look up, it would start; parents at the counter demanding meetings, a kid having a seizure, meetings with a dis-trict committee. . . . I would fill out my calendar every Sunday night with meetings for the week and by Tuesday, the only time I ever had to plan anything was early in the morning. I never got out to the classrooms, ex-cept to conduct evaluation observations. Even then I did half-hearted work with the veteran teachers because I knew I wasn't going to get rid of them. The observations felt like an interruption to what I really needed to get done back in the office. I figured the rush was simply the way it was. My colleagues at other schools would commiserate with me about the speed of the day and the importance of the erupting problems we dealt with at the same time.

When I was asked by the superintendent to reform a middle school, I found the same problems coming to me at the same pace; it did not mat-ter that the school was half the size of the high school I had just left. There were still tons of things to pull me in twenty directions and classroom ob-servations were the last thing on my list of priorities. I think that is one of the biggest problems where curricular leadership is concerned. Principals are supposed to be sheriffs, social workers, and therapists, *and* empower teachers to become better. I found that I had to manipulate the meetings I had set in the day or skip classroom observations with veteran teachers because there was a project I needed to finish or a district meeting that popped up. It seemed to me that ultimately I played with my scheduled classroom time the most. Eventually I felt out of touch with my class-rooms.

I finally decided one day that my time in classrooms was not going to suffer. If I made some parents irritated or even the district office, I didn't care. I was sick of not being able to devote the time I wanted to working with classroom teachers. So in July I filled out my personal calendar for the whole year. I scheduled in red indelible ink four classroom visits for every member of my staff. I did not necessarily inform the teachers what day I had them calendared for, but I let my secretary know that if my daily calendar had a meeting blocked out in red, it was non-negotiable: I would not miss it. At first it was difficult; some people were irritated at my inflexibility where classroom observations were concerned. Even I was frustrated that I had to turn down some things I liked to do, such as speak at the Rotary Club. But by the end of the year, it seemed that my teachers respected me in a different way and I felt like I had a handle of what really is going on in the classrooms of my school.

Being disciplined and sticking to what is calendared will help you meet your goals of reinforcing your values and expectations throughout your school constituencies. Planning ahead is the key. Find a time before the chaos of the year begins and think about what is important to you to devote your time to. Then plan your yearly schedule around your goals. To get a better idea of specifics, review the list in figure 3.2.

PRIORITIZING CLASSROOM VISITS AND EVALUATIONS

The next section of this chapter deals specifically with how one assesses the teaching staff he or she is working with. Begin an assessment by making a point at the start of the year (the first two weeks) to get into every teacher's classroom and "pop in." A pop-in is simply a way to say hello, get some face time with students and teachers, and make people feel welcome. On a more pedagogical level, pop-ins are great as they ensure a sense of connectedness and accountability between the principal and the teacher. Because you are "the boss," your presence will intimidate some teachers. Do what you can to set them at ease but remember it is a good thing for your staff to understand that you will be in their classroom. The more you pop in, the more accustomed the teachers will become to seeing you and the less threatening you will be.

When you pop in, say hello and proceed to sit with the students and participate in whatever the lesson is. Ask students what they are doing. Ask them what they are learning. Then move over to the teacher to say hello or ask how the lesson is going. While you are chatting, note the tone of the class. Ask yourself, "Are all the students on task? What is the teacher doing to ensure they are all on task? Is the lesson relevant? Are students watching a movie? If so, is this a valuable exercise? What is the benefit of the lesson?" Think about your answers as they relate to the value statement you created about good, excellent, and acceptable teachers.

When you leave the classroom, check your gut and decide what kind of class you just visited. Three pop-ins per one teacher at various times of the day will help solidify if you are seeing a good, excellent, or acceptable teacher. You may find that you have some unacceptable teachers from the pop-ins. Once you have decided from this brief snapshot, prioritize who will be evaluated first from your pop-ins. Make the unacceptable teachers a top priority. Be mindful to check with your personnel department as there are timelines for nonrenewing a teacher. The mediocre teachers who squeak through the educational system usually get by because their principal failed to meet the union-negotiated evaluation timelines. If the timelines for evaluation are not met—usually a teacher is safe from being nonrenewed. The next on your priority list for the observation process is the acceptable category and the good, followed by the excellent teachers.

If you share evaluating duties with assistants, divide up the staff fairly in terms of who gets to evaluate whom, but consider taking the most difficult evaluations for yourself. For all the teachers who fall in the unacceptable category, classroom visits are nonnegotiable in your calendar. Stick to your scheduled visits and make sure to follow the procedures in your district's bargaining agreement. Usually, a school district will host an in-service on teacher evaluation for principals in August. If that does not happen, make sure to set an appointment with your human resources director to understand the appropriate policies and procedures.

THE PRECONFERENCE

Once you have established who you will be evaluating and when, calendar in the preobservation conference and send memos out to your staff informing them what date and time they will be meeting with you. It is a very good idea to hold a faculty meeting to present to staff what a preconference with you will look like. At this meeting, set your expectations. Talk to staff about what you look for in a lesson plan. Following is

Prioritizing Your Calendar and Scheduling Ideas

- Use colored pencils or markers to code your entries, i.e.. red is nonnegotiable time, green is flexible time, district meetings and events are orange, community events are blue.

- As you think about your professional goals for the year, load in all meetings and events related to your goal in your calendar in red.

- Dedicate the first and last two weeks of each semester to visiting every classroom for at least ten minutes to say hello or wish student happy holidays. Make these appointments nonnegotiable. Not only is this good PR, it will help you see teachers understand that you will be there to see how they wind down their semester.

- Schedule the four days of teaching and stick to it.

- Schedule four lunches in the year in which you help serve the lunch. (Leonard Sweeney, a principal in Phoenix, grilled hamburgers for the entire school at the end of every grading period.)

- Schedule four times a year in which you sit in the teachers lounge through the entire lunch cycle and listen to what teachers have to say. Bring your lunch or better yet, have some treats for the teachers available.

- Schedule teacher appreciation day and the days beforehand for you to make arrangements to honor them; maybe you will deliver a cookie and coffee to each teacher while they are in class.

Figure 3.2. Tips for Prioritizing Your Calendar and Scheduling Ideas

- Schedule extra pop-in (ten minutes or less) visits to teachers' classrooms that you are concerned about. It lets them know you are watching and allows you to see what is going on.

- Schedule visits to schools events that you need to " be there ... be seen ... and be gone..." such as basketball games, dances, science fairs, plays, concerts etc.

- Schedule one hour a week to write positive individual notes to staff members, recognizing good work; keep a list so everyone gets two notes a year from you.

- Schedule one day a year that you wear casual clothes and be a student for a day.

- Schedule four lunches (or beers) with other principals in your district to build relationships and "check in."

- Schedule monthly early breakfast meetings with your office staff, nurse, and school counselors to check the status of the administrative offices.

- Schedule one day a year to visit another school and shadow a colleague just to see how they do things differently than you; return the favor and host a shadow principal for a day.

- Schedule a 'principal for a day' that is a community partner.

- Schedule a public community activity for you to raise awareness in your school, i.e.- work the drive through at the local fast-food restaurant, or help at the day care center, or work in the hair salon to help raise money or books or community support.

Figure 3.2 (*continued*)

- Schedule planning days for your faculty professional development so that you don't plan things at the last minute.

- Schedule, if possible, a retreat day for your administrative team to set goals and reflect on the year.

- Schedule two individual, private chats with every single person on staff every year. One in the fall, and one in the spring semester. This builds relationships and lets you check in with what they are doing personally and professionally. Listen to your staff members during the meeting. Take notes if necessary to remember details.

Figure 3.2 (continued)

a list of what the most basic lesson plan should include and a brief definition of each of the aspects.

1. **The Objective**—The objective is what the teacher wants the students to be able to do by the end of the lesson. An effective formula for writing objectives includes a statement about students being able to demonstrate an understanding of a concept by doing something. For example, "Students will be able to demonstrate an understanding of the four major parts of a cell by drawing them and labeling them on scratch paper." Or, "Students will be able to identify the first ten amendments of the U.S. Constitution by identifying them within a list of many amendments."
2. **Materials Used**—This is the opportunity for the teacher to explain to you what he or she will be using in class. This section does not mean that the teacher must use newfangled gadgets; chalk and paper are acceptable materials in many creative contexts.
3. **Opening Set**—This is where the teacher begins to explain how he or she is going to teach the lesson. The opening set is the very first thing the teacher does to catch the students' attention and make them think. Curriculum specialists and philosophers like John Dewey would also argue that it is at this place where it is most important that the teacher do something to weave the lesson

into students' prior knowledge. For example, a teacher whose objective is to have students demonstrate an understanding of the effects of adrenaline on the human body would write in his or her lesson plan in the opening set section: "I plan to ask all of my students to close their eyes and think of a time when they felt so angry or scared that they could feel their heart beating. Then I will have them open their eyes and ask the students why they think their heart beat became so prominent."

4. **Method of Delivery**—It is here that you find most teachers saying things like, "Group discussion, small group activities, scavenger hunts, experiments, computer research, and guest speakers."

5. **Assessment**—Perhaps the most important section is assessment. Often teachers think they are engaged in "authentic teaching." What authentic teaching means is that teachers are really teaching something valuable and relevant to students. The discussions among politicians and educators concerning what is valuable and relevant have fueled the national controversies as well as state-level legislation concerning standardized tests (for a more in-depth look at this issue, read *The Manufactured Crisis* by David Berliner and B. Biddle). For the purposes of this section, principals need to be mindful that the teachers often truly believe that they are delivering a legitimate lesson. Unfortunately, it can be tempting to forget what is age appropriate and valuable in a classroom. Cooking in class is the longtime example that curriculum experts use to explain how one can confuse an authentic lesson. Simultaneously, one must remember that a true assessment means that the student has to do something physically to demonstrate his or her newly acquired knowledge. For example, a lesson in omelet making in a high school culinary arts class, in which at the end of class students make omelets and eat them, is quite appropriate. Students making Christmas ornaments in a fifth-grade homeroom class after lunch because it is the last week of school before holiday break is not an authentic lesson. The lesson would gain authenticity if the fifth graders had just finished reading a book about the history of ornaments and wrote a reflection paragraph that was now posted on a bulletin board in the classroom. Again, it is the point of the assessment section to help

teachers reflect on what they are doing in class and how they are assessing their students' progress.

6. **Alignment to State Standards**—This is the section where the teacher can communicate to the principal, as well as to the community, what he or she is doing in class that is related to the educational grade-level standards set by the state in which they work. What is nice about this section in a lesson plan is that it forces teachers to think about their teaching in general and in specifics and how it relates to mandated educational standards. It also empowers teachers to actually read the standards. A typical answer to this section would include, "This lesson meets educational grade-level objective 3.1, 3.4, and 5.1 of the state standards for grade five." Here again this section provides a wonderful opportunity to discuss with staff in a faculty meeting what the state- and district-level expectations are for schools. It also allows you, the principal, to say that your staff has aligned the curriculum to state standards as evidenced by teachers' lesson plans.

When you review teachers' lesson plans, look to see if the assessment matches the objective. It is not appropriate to say that students' knowledge will be assessed the next week on a quiz. Authentic assessment of a student learning should happen right at the end of the lesson. It is not appropriate or accurate to understand that students will be assessed by questions asked to the entire class. One or two students may answer the questions, so how does the teacher know that all of the students have achieved the objective? The most desirable assessment usually involves students writing something individually such as a reflective paragraph or sentence and then handing it in to the teacher. In turn, that teacher should review the brief reflections and make quick comments back to his or her students. The reflections also help the teacher monitor and adjust his or her instruction. If the student "didn't get it," the teacher needs to retry the lesson again the next day.

Another thing to look for in lesson plans is the variety of methods a teacher will use. Does that teacher change his or her approach or is this a monotonous class for students? Finally, consider if the objective is age and grade level appropriate. If you think the answer is no, ask the teacher to explain what he or she believes his or her objective to be.

After you review the lesson plan and make notes to yourself, decide on three things to focus on when you have your preobservation conference. When you start the preobservation conference, make sure that you are both sitting at a table together or in a nonthreatening place other than you on one side of your desk and the teacher on the other. Remember, this is still a somewhat intimidating experience for even veteran teachers because they have never been evaluated by you. They are not sure of your expectations and if they fit them. After welcoming the teacher, tell them you reviewed their plan and ask them to go over it with you. Ask questions as they are talking. Affirm the teacher first with two positive comments about the plan. Then approach your concern. Most teachers forget the affirmations and concentrate only on the concerns so make sure you lower their level of threat by affirming the strengths you see. If you can, weave some positive statements about what you have already seen in their classroom and then ask if they would like you to look for anything in particular to give them feedback on. Then confirm the observation date and time and tell them you are looking forward to coming to class.

THE OBSERVATION

The most important thing to remember concerning the observation visit is the seriousness of the event. It does not matter how jaded or confident teachers appear, this is their moment to demonstrate their expertise to their supervisor. All teachers are also a little nervous because they want everything to be perfect.

An unwritten rule for principals is that they can be late or leave meetings early because their schedules are so crammed and they are the boss. However, this axiom excludes classroom visits. Honor the sanctity of your role as the curriculum leader and be on time. This is one place that you cannot afford to be late. Your actions during the visit quickly educate your staff about who you are as a leader. It is here you need to pay particular attention to frontstage behavior. Many principals make the mistake of thinking that because they have told the teacher they are terrific and that they intended to give a good evaluation that this excuses an observation that has minimal effort. By giving a substandard effort toward the evaluation process, you lose credibility with your staff, and even the excellent teachers that you assumed gave you loyalty will crucify you in the lounge. Why? Because even though you said they were great on paper you did not give them the professional respect they deserve by thoughtfully engaging in their evaluation.

Bring a clipboard with a legal pad on it to the classroom and something to write with. Also have a watch so that you can see the time clearly. Many teachers will ask you when you enter where you want to sit. Choose a seat in the back and try to make your entry as nonintrusive as possible. Pop-ins are the time for you to be larger than life and play with the students. Observation visits are the time for you to be invisible and carefully watch what is going on.

SCRIPTING A LESSON

There are myriad ways to script a lesson. Your district may have some system that you are required to follow. Figure 3.3 demonstrates the down-and-dirty approach that this author found most effective.

Here is an example of a principal's scripting notes using the down-and-dirty method (figure 3.4).

ANALYZING SCRIPTING NOTES

Once you have left the classroom with the scripted notes, take two minutes (even if it is on the sidewalk outside the classroom) and write down any additional comments you had about your visit, things like the rapport you saw between the students and teacher or maybe questions you have for the teacher such as "Why did you pick this lesson?" Usually principals analyze their script notes when they have a moment to concentrate and fill out the teacher evaluation document. That moment is usually hours or days after the observation. Writing quick notes about general observations when you leave a classroom allows you to archive details that might be forgotten without a moment to reflect. In figure

The Basics of Scripting

- Write on the upper right-hand side the teachers name, the date, the class, and the time.
- Use the left-hand margin already delineated by the printing on the paper to notate the time. When the lesson begins, notate the time.
- After you have written the first notation of time, write down a description of what you see on the blackboard.
- Next, write down what the teacher is doing for their opening set.
- When the set is finished and the teacher is moving on to something else, write down the time on the left margin. Moving to something else is called a transition. Effective teachers at any grade level have regular and consistent transitions.
- Write down when questions are asked.
- Note who the teacher questions, and write down the names of the students.
- Write down the type of method used, i.e., small group, partners, etc.
- When it gets a little difficult for you to concentrate, write down in the right margin how the classroom is decorated. Is current student work posted? Is there a sense of theme and order in the classroom environment?
- Write down what kind of discipline you see. Does the teacher maintain an orderly classroom environment?
- Note when you see students off- task; include their names if possible and the exact time you observed this.
- Note when you see the closing activity and the time.
- Note the kind of assessment the teacher used.

Figure 3.3. The Basics of Scripting

3.5 is a list of global questions to help with scripting analysis and how they are relevant to all evaluation instruments.

Once you have analyzed your notes, prepare for the postobservation conference by choosing three things concerning your visit that you will praise the teacher on and one thing to suggest to the teacher for growth. This can be difficult as sometimes there are five things that a teacher should focus on. For purposes of this discussion, a ratio of three positives to one challenge is appropriate. If your scripting reveals so many

Mr. Shane, grade ten

3rd period Social Studies

12/10/03

10:02 am

Opening set   Good morning… What happened on the news last night? Karen?
Yep… Sadaam Hussein was captured by US forces… What do you
think about that? Mark…? (also gets answers and opinions from
John, Mathew, and Corey). Well, today we are going to look at how
Hussein's capture is related to the presidential election….

10:10

Delivery   You need to get into groups of three and look through these news
papers and on the internet for news article related to this weekend
events. See what the media has to say about this and the election. We
will get together in twenty minutes to talk about it.   Students get into
groups. Sarah is sleeping in the back row. "Sarah. are you going to
sleep all day? Or would you like to join us?" Sarah wakes up and
gets on task. Shaner circulates around the room.

10:30   "OK… let's see what we found…. Mandy? Erin? Samantha?" Corey
asks, "Why don't we just kill Hussein?" Shaner answers with a
description of the Geneva convention and the Hague.

No current student work displayed. Bulletin board in back has sports articles and
covers from Rolling Stone Magazine posted. Room is clean. Students have a good
rapport with teacher. Jerry and Darious were throwing notes back and forth during
discussion.

10:50   End of class bell rings. " OK, we didn't get to finish our goal for
today so for tomorrow be ready to finish the discussion. Have a good
day."

Figure 3.4.   Example of a Principal's Scripting Notes

inadequacies in the classroom, you may want to consider putting the
teacher on a plan of improvement or moving to nonrenew the teacher.
Chapter 5 discusses these options.

Fill out the district evaluation instrument and do not be afraid to write
in the comments section suggestions for improvement. Use the phrase

Scripting Questions

- Were all the parts of a minimal lesson covered: Opening set, Delivery of instruction, Assessment?
- What kind of questioning strategies were used? Were all of the questions knowledge level or were there more complicated analysis and synthesis questions?
- Did the teacher only call on girls? Only call on boys?
- Did the teacher call on anyone sitting in the back of the room?
- Did the teacher treat students with dignity?
- Did the actual lesson match the lesson plan?
- What were the transition times? Was there an even flow? Was too much time spent on one activity, thus throwing off the lesson?
- What did this lesson have to do with state standards?
- Was this an authentic lesson versus something that was entertaining?
- Was the assessment authentic?
- What did the classroom feel like? Was it inviting?
- Was student work displayed?
- Did the teacher connect with the students? Were the students engaged and on task?
- Was the teacher passionate about the subject matter?
- Was the teacher able to empower students to connect the lesson to the real world?
- What bothered me, the observer, the most during the lesson?
- What did I like the most during the lesson?
- Was there a sense of discipline and order in the class?
- Did the students treat the teacher with respect?

Figure 3.5.   Global Questions to Help with Scripting Analysis

"Continue to focus on . . ." when writing a challenge. This verbiage soft-ens the language and eases the reader into reflecting on what you are say-ing. As for the positives, start compliments with phrases such as "Mr. Shane is a great addition to our staff. His strengths include . . ." If you make the choice not to give a suggestion for improvement, you are telling your staff that they do not need to improve on anything. You also are contributing to a false sense of perfection among your teaching staff. Be aware of what happens when you give teachers all perfect scores on their evaluations. You may experience teachers coming to you complaining that they got a "4" instead of a perfect "5" score for bulletin boards. As a culture, educators are often the first people to find it difficult to reflect legitimately upon our strengths and weaknesses. By perpetuating the myth of perfection in your staff, you also perpetuate mediocrity and a lack of self-reflection. Ultimately, this affects the quality of experiences that your students receive.

THE POSTOBSERVATION CONFERENCE

Here again, be on time and be prepared. Know that your teacher will be nervous. Start the conference in a neutral spot in your office; do not have your teacher sit on one side of your desk and you on the other. Begin the conference by asking the teacher how he or she thought the lesson went. Be quiet and let him or her talk. If the teacher says "fine" and nothing else, then respond by saying "What about the lesson was fine?" Use probing questions such as "Tell me more about that . . ." to help that teacher really reflect on what happened. Interject as appropriate concerning the strengths you saw. In most cases the teacher will identify for you the challenges or weaknesses that you observed. For example, in figure 3.5, the script notes in Mr. Shane's class reveal that there was no assessment of student learning and that there were twenty minutes of group work. There might also be a question as to how the objective is related to state standards for tenth graders. Also, there were some notes concerning how his room looked. If Mr. Shane were in a postconference with his principal, it might go something like this:

Principal: How did the lesson go?

Mr. Shane: Well I felt like time got away from us. They were just so excited about the capture of Saddam Hussein. Then they wanted to know why we don't just kill him. It seemed a ripe time to discuss world politics and before I knew it the bell rang.

Principal: Yes, I saw that. But I also saw that it is clear that you are passionate about politics and that the kids were interested in what you were saying. Tell me about Darius. He is quite a card.

Mr. Shane: Yeah, I saw him passing notes, I just didn't want to interrupt the flow of the discussion.

Principal: Is there a way you could have kept him on task?

Mr. Shane: Well, I guess I could have stopped the entire class to reprimand him—I just did not want to waste class time.

Principal: I see your point. . . . Tell me more about wasting class time. Where is it that you think the clock got away from you?

Mr. Shane: Well . . . we spent a lot of time on the Hague. . . .

Principal: I am wondering what would have happened if instead of giving the students twenty minutes to look up articles in groups if you had given them ten.

Mr. Shane: Maybe that would have made a difference.

Principal: I also wanted to mention that it is clear the kids like you and enjoy your class. I think your student rapport is definitely a strength. I liked the *Rolling Stone* covers on the bulletin board. Any chance you could balance that out by putting some student work up as well?

Mr. Shane: Yes, I could do that.

Principal: You know I also like the fact that you are getting our kids to think. I thought your objective was an interesting one and it matches your lesson plan. However, because your transition time was a little sluggish you did not get time to assess whether they learned anything about how the capture of Saddam Hussein impacts the presidential election. If there was one thing I could encourage you to do it would be to watch those transitions, so that you can actually assess if your students met your objective. I also want to reiterate again that your students love coming to your class. You do a great deal of extracurricular work for our school with your coaching. It is a pleasure to work with you. If you look at the evaluation instrument I have given you these scores in these areas. In the comments section I have written that you are a team-oriented colleague, that you are popular with our students, and that you are passionate about the subject you teach. You can also see that I have encouraged you to be conscious of your transition times to ensure that there is an opportunity for you to assess whether your students met the objective of your lesson. Are there any questions I can answer for you?

Mr. Shane: No, not at the moment.

Principal: Well if you think of any let me know. I need you to sign this form you received with your evaluation, and I am glad we got a chance to talk. Thanks for coming in.

What this dialogue shows is that on the evaluation instrument, there is only one point of reflection. But during the conference, the principal raised several things for the teacher to think about. How did the principal select the one point of reflection to write down? By going back to the list of values about teachers that he had created for himself. The principal knows that authentic student assessment is much more important than what is on a bulletin board.

CHAPTER 3 INSTANT REPLAY: TEACHING AND TEACHERS

1. You cannot articulate your beliefs about teaching until you innately know them.
2. Beware of how the pressure to fill an empty teaching slot blurs your standards of excellence in the classroom.
3. Not all teachers are perfect when hired. Invest the appropriate amount of time to give them support in their first years on staff.
4. Clear, consistent communication is the only way to demonstrate your expectations concerning excellence in the classroom.
5. Treat the evaluation process with respect—stick to timelines and be on time.
6. During an evaluation conference, praise three things for every one deficiency noted.
7. Be sensitive to how teachers feel during the evaluation process. Enhance and maintain staff members' dignity when reinforcing expectations.
8. Model a willingness to increase your knowledge of the science of curriculum and the art of teaching.
9. Don't "fake it." No one respects pretense or false omniscience in a leader.
10. Choose one area to focus on when writing a teaching evaluation report. Talk about three, but write up only one.

4

VITAL STATS
AND
THE PLAYERS'
PROGRAM GUIDE

Coach Jerome returned from the rest room at the back of the restaurant to find her two assistant coaches in a heated discussion . . . again. Tanisha Franklin's arms were waving around when she practically screamed, "Yeah, Yeah, we all know Lebron James is the new 'go to guy,' but he's still young. He needs to be seasoned. He still doesn't know his role yet. No matter how smooth he is, his youth still sells him out in his interviews."

"You have got to be kidding!" Brenda Scott snapped back. "No doubt about it that the young man is a franchise player. But you have to give an investment like that some time to develop. Besides, where is the rest of his team? You know, Kobe had Shaq. And Duncan had Robinson. Every team has a 'go to guy,' but greatness takes more than one player. You have to have completeness. Sometimes it's the sixth man that brings a team to the next level."

Tanisha thought for a while and then said, "One person can't do it alone. Even a franchise player has to have support from the people around him. Think about Michael Jordan, he was an all-around player. What made the Bulls great for so many years was that he was supported by a bunch of players who understood their role. Jordan is still my all-time favorite. The man had heart. He played for the love of the game. He is still the greatest."

Coach Jerome sat down at the table and interrupted:

Ladies I want you to think about the importance of the last thing Tanisha said. No one ever has a team of all Michael Jordans. That is where the art of coaching comes in. The bottom line is that a team comes together because of how they are coached. You can have a team of all-stars, and if they don't have vision or a sense of team—it all falls apart. Some coaches build that sense through fear and some through love. The fine line between nurturing and kicking a player in the butt is where true leadership comes into play. Good coaching isn't always about growling at your players to hold them accountable every second. By the same token, it isn't about telling everyone every day that they are the greatest. I don't think the ability to do both is related to gender. Think about Pat Summit. Do you think the Lady Vols would have six national championships under her leadership if she had not figured out exactly how to pull the greatest efforts from each of her players? Or look at John Wooden from UCLA. The man has ten national championships under his belt. Somehow, I don't think that guy is always screaming at practice and throwing his clipboard around.

The key is knowing your players and finding different ways to push their buttons in terms of motivation and inspiration. Ultimately, the great coaches are also teachers. Take Phil Jackson, for example. You know what he does? He assigns specific pieces of literature to each of his players. I read in the paper last week that Shaq credits his new outlook on strategy to reading a copy of *The Art of War* that Coach Jackson gave him. You would think that reading and coaching don't really go together, but they do, because part of motivating someone to improve is understanding how to teach them something new.

"But coach, how do you know a new recruit?" Tanisha asked. "What if you are new to the team and you are stuck with the people that the coach before you recruited? You can't connect with people you don't know. You end up taking a whole season just to figure out how those players work."

"True." Coach Jerome responded:

But that is also where experience comes into play. Just like when you and Brenda were talking about guards. Brenda said Lebron was a franchise player. Well, you knew exactly what a franchise player was. You understood immediately what that category meant because you understand the game of basketball. Or if I describe a player to you as a showboat, do you know immediately what I mean? Of course you do. You even know what it means if a complete stranger tells you that a player has no heart. Like all other coaches, you have developed a kind of program guide in your head that describes different types of players through your work on the court.

Experience, training, and visits to coaching clinics teach us how to deal with these different types of athletes. For example, at the clinic in Knoxville last year, we heard that assistant coach talk about how sometimes you let your showboats loose on the court as a reward for hard work and sometimes you rein them in because they are forgetting that they are part of a team. In terms of leading, you can motivate people faster when you can connect with them faster. And you can connect with them faster when you start to understand who they are. That program guide inside your head is a great tool to help you size up the folks you don't know. It isn't a hundred percent accurate, but it is a great starting point to understanding the general categories that different people sort of lend themselves to.

THE PROGRAM GUIDE FOR TEACHERS

Coaches and principals have the same issues when they start to work with a franchise or school that is new to them. This section is a reference guide to those different types of teachers and contains some brief suggestions on how to understand and work with them.

The Rookie

Rookies, to most people, are obviously those teachers new to the profession. The mistake many rookies (as well as their seasoned colleagues) make is to assume that once the first year in the classroom is completed, they no longer need the support or expectations that are afforded new teachers. Most rookies are not only young professionally, they are young period. This means that there is a certain degree of insecurity and immaturity that comes with their raw talent and energy. It takes an extra effort on the part of a school's administrative staff to ensure that there are mentors available for rookies. The first step for any principal to take, in terms of supporting rookies, is to extend the definition of rookie to include those teachers in their second or third year in the classroom. Most rookies complete their first year with some sense of classroom discipline and some sense of how the year flows and that is about all. The two years following a rookie year are when teachers really look at themselves and develop a philosophy of teaching, classroom discipline, and colleague-ship.

Principals should take the time to assign a mentor teacher if possible to rookies when they are first hired. Appropriate mentors are other teachers who are role models in terms of instruction and classroom management. It is important to select mentors who are willing to build a relationship with rookies. The worst possible action in terms of mentoring is to read a list of mentors and rookies at the beginning of the year faculty meeting and then do nothing else to foster a relationship between these two colleagues.

The mentor–protégé relationship is something that relies on chemistry, as well as both parties' willingness to participate in the relationship. Ultimately the goal should be that the mentor and rookie have the kind of relationship where the rookie feels that the mentor is a safe person to go to with his or her insecurities and to seek advice. This will not happen without efforts made to build a relationship between the two colleagues. Successful mentor programs include activities during initial teacher orientation in August that allow each person to get to know one another and find similar interests and values. Mentors and protégés need support. Their relationship cannot grow without opportunities for them to talk with each other. And when school starts, the odds are that both will become so wrapped up in their own classrooms that they will not seek each other out. Support these folks by planning and hosting regular (once a month) book or coffee talks with mentors and protégés to discuss issues related to the school year. Appropriate themes would be classroom discipline, professional and personal development, creation of a plan for graduate school, handling stress, dealing with parents, the evaluation process, standardized testing, and closing down the classroom at the end of the year. Also allow yourself a meeting just for mentors to explain what your expectations are of them. Talk to your mentor teachers about the many ways they will represent you and the school's vision to new staff. Teach your mentors what is important for them to share with their protégés. Remind them that if they have concerns or questions about their protégé, they need to tell you. The object of this whole program is to provide support for rookie teachers to grow into successful, confident veterans. This will happen in a manner that is directly related to the amount of planning and attention you give to your mentors and rookies.

The Endless Well of Need

This kind of teacher is different than a rookie who is supposed to be a little needy and insecure. This kind of teacher is also different than the teacher who is experiencing change because he or she is tackling a new subject matter or grade level. This teacher is not a colleague who is experiencing a traumatic personal event such as divorce, or death in the family, or personal stress of some kind. This particular type of teacher stands out because no matter how much you praise him or her, how much you empower him or her, it will never be enough. These are the folks who whine that they are never appreciated. Some of these folks are effective in the classroom and some are not. These are the employees who will actively seek you out to be their therapists. And like all good bartenders, priests, and parents, in many ways a principal is a therapist.

As the matriarch or patriarch of your school you should tell people the door to your office is always open; and you need to mean it. For many, you are a conduit to various support and social services that your employees need. However, there is a fine line between providing counsel, support, and interventions and to unwittingly participating in a codependent relationship. Principal Adrian Worthington offers this example:

> I had this teacher, Rhonda, who was in her second year at our school. She had been in the profession for five years. She would often pop into my office to say hello and I liked her. And frankly she was good for my ego. She sought my advice and I was flattered by that. After her first successful year at our school, we decided to create a Welcome Center for students and their families new to the campus. We realized that we would need to move a teacher to this position. So I asked Rhonda if she would like this opportunity. She was very excited about the leadership opportunity and agreed. After a few initial planning sessions, I let Rhonda do as she pleased with the center. I was so proud of her efforts that I gave her a sterling silver fountain pen to thank her in early October. As the year progressed, other projects took my attention. Because the Welcome Center was running smoothly, I simply did not meet with Rhonda as much. In December, Rhonda asked my secretary for a meeting with me because she had some concerns. When we met, I assumed we would be talking about the Welcome Center. Wrong. Rhonda was concerned because I did not say "hello" to her as I used to. So I explained I was busy and reminded her that she was one of my superstars. . . . That I appreciated her efforts. . . . I reminded her that I even gave her a fountain pen to recognize her efforts. She said "OK, but it is not the same." After that meeting ended, a month went by and then Rhonda wanted to meet with me again. So we met. And it was the same thing. She did not feel valued. I again reminded her that we had just completed her teacher evaluation and it was stellar. Even after the meeting I would try to pop in to the Welcome Center to say hello. But then one day I realized that I was now going to see Rhonda because of guilt. No matter what I did, Rhonda wanted more. I gave her an award

at the end of the year for being a leader and contributing to the school. It was not enough. She always had another reason to request a meeting that ended up in her telling me I wasn't giving her enough attention. Frankly, I got sick of this. I couldn't win; I would give her attention and she would want more. And if I did not give her what she needed, she would try and throw a guilt trip. When I brought her behavior to her attention, she got angry and then gossiped about me in the faculty lounge. Naturally, I started giving her the least attention possible. I think if I had just drawn some parameters earlier, we would not have ended in this weird cycle.

The lessons from Rhonda parallel the Parable of the Marble Jar. Essentially the idea in this story is that the principal, like all leaders of organizations, is responsible as caretaker to meet with folks. At each meeting, an employee has a need or request that can be symbolized as a marble. So our principal spends all day, say, handing out marbles from his or her jar in the form of support, empathy, and attention. The caveat is this: A principal has only so many marbles in his or her jar. If he or she is not careful, the principal will lose all his or her marbles. And no one needs a principal who has lost all his or her marbles.

Yes, the above pun is cheesy, but its point is not diminished by its sarcasm. Every day the principalship requires you to give away pieces of yourself in terms of emotion and attention. Give yourself permission to draw boundaries and watch out for those employees who turn to you to define their self-concept. Remember, your job is not to make everyone feel good. Your job is to ensure that students and teachers are empowered to be successful in the classroom.

The Lone Wolf

Of all the members on staff, this teacher is the hardest to get to know. Many of these teachers are veterans, although that is not always the case. Lone wolves want to be left alone. Sometimes it is because their teaching job is secondary to something else, such as a side business like real estate. Or they might be introverted and relish solitude. Or it could be that they like to avoid the extra work that being part of a teaching community demands. Because lone wolves are so invisible, principals need to make extra efforts to connect professionally with them. Pop-ins are especially important with lone wolves as a tool to help reinforce your expectations and parameters. Singling out a lone wolf in a faculty meeting will not endear him or her to you. Lone wolves like to be invisible and do their own thing. It is hard to get buy-in from these folks because they usually are not included in the system anyway. The best way to build a relationship with them is to force yourself to be in their classrooms regularly and to give them reflective honest feedback about what you see going on. Principals often ignore lone wolves because they see them as something of a benign member of campus. Do not fall for this common mistake. Ignoring lone wolves only reinforces to them that they can stay invisible both personally and in terms of accountability.

The Big Shot

Big shots are those folks that have been there, done that, and know it all. Moreover, they have a need to make sure that you and everyone else in their proximity realize they know it all. Often these teachers are very good in the classroom. The problem is that they are *so sure* they are *so good* at their jobs that change is essentially unnecessary in their minds (along with any other ideas you, the principal, may have). Sarah Jones, an assistant principal, offers this example of what it is like to deal with a big shot:

> Our school has a huge number of kids who are primarily Spanish speakers. There are so many that now we have them mainstreamed into classes where the teachers and students speak only English. One of our teachers found me in the hallway after we put some Spanish-speaking students in her room and told me she was directing her entire class to color and watch a cartoon for the rest of the day. When I asked her why, she informed me that her job was to teach, not to take care of kids who could not even speak English. I told her that our ESL teachers could provide her with a list of appropriate student activities. She refused to meet with them, saying that she was a trained teacher and that "those kids" were not in her job description. This woman was something: She even had the brass to tell our superintendent in a public faculty meeting that she found a "general malaise" among her students and that it made it totally difficult for her to do her job. Can you believe that? I mean her job is to motivate kids. If her kids weren't motivated, then that is her fault. This teacher thought she was all that and a bag of chips. She just walked around here like she was the queen of the prom.

The difficulty in dealing with big shots is their ego. It will get in the way of their empathy and teamwork and will try your patience. The secret to garnering buy-in from a big shot is to help them understand that any sort of change is basically their idea. If you have a problem and know what action you are going to take to solve it, invest time into educating your big shots about the problem and why your answer is the only viable one. Big shots learn slowly, so expose them over and over again through faculty meetings and discussions to the problem at hand and the direction the school is going to take. Big shots are usually leaders among their peers, so the buy-in to your solution increases dramatically when they buy into your ideas. Be careful as to how and where you decide to educate big shots. If you choose large faculty meetings, know that the big shot will delight in challenging you in public. Be prepared by strategizing what questions he or she will have so that you will already have appropriate answers. Big shots delight in finding the flaws to your ideas and thus showing their colleagues that they are a bigger shot than the commander in chief. Be wary of too many one-on-one meetings or grade-level meetings with your big shot about issues and strategies. This approach may look to the faculty like you have lost some of your perceived power because you are deferring to the big shot.

Big shots will delight in circling the grammatical errors in your faculty newsletters and handing them back to you. Do not be intimidated by such tactics. These are simply efforts to let you know that this person is really threatened by your positional power. In some cases, you can earn a big shot's respect by being honest and loyal and acting with integrity. Other times, you will just have to live with the big shot.

In either case, the key is to strategize how this type of teacher will seek to engage in power struggles with you. Be prepared to meet his or her questions, barbs, or corrections head-on and with dignity. Anger is never the key with a big shot. When you get angry with them, you lose, and they know it. Keep your cool at all times and when they ask you a difficult question in public, meant to make you look foolish or stupid, respond by either saying you will find the answer and get back to them or use light humor to deflect the moment. However, be careful with your humor. Big shots do not like to be one-upped in public and these types of folks have long memories and can carry grudges. Your acerbic remark about a big shot in a faculty meeting could result in all sorts of teachers' lounge politics that will make your job all the more difficult. Ultimately, you want a big shot to feel respected, but you also want them to understand your expectations. Do not expect these folks to like you. Usually they do not like anyone in positions of authority because they feel threatened.

The Movie Coach

These teachers are the folks who seem to always have a movie going on every time you walk into their classroom. The first question to ask yourself if you notice lots of movies in a class is "What is the purpose?" It is possible that this teacher enjoys using media in his or her lessons and has put a great deal of energy into coordinating media presentations and pop culture experiences with authentic instruction. It is also possible that this teacher has discovered that showing movies is a convenient way to pass the time through an instructional day. The best way to tackle the challenge of a classroom inundated with movies is to schedule in your calendar many pop-ins at different times of day over a period of several weeks. When you visit the classroom, also look to see if the students are asleep or if they are engaged in some activity that requires them to interact with the video presentation.

If you have decided that you have a movie coach in your midst, address your concerns with this teacher through the evaluation system. Ask your teacher to explain in his or her lesson plans how the movies benefit the learning of students and how they are related to standardized test-preparation efforts.

Another thing to consider is why there are so many movies in class. Is the teacher a coach or club sponsor currently struggling through a hectic season of extracurricular activities? Is the teacher dealing with some other stressor that leaves him or her feeling a need to spend classroom time doing something else rather than delivering instruction? Is this scenario constant or is it temporary?

Finally, consider what you really can do about this situation. If the teacher is a long-term veteran who has done this for years, do you have the time to invest in a long and stressful evaluation process? Can this teacher be coached into moving into a different type of class or set of responsibilities on campus? Perhaps you might share with your teacher that if his or her extracurricular responsibilities are in the way of his or her classroom responsibilities, you are in a position to change the teacher's assignment as a coach or sponsor.

If you ignore this situation, can you afford to let the rest of your staff see that you turn a blind eye to an essentially feckless classroom? In many instances, the honest answer you find in your heart to this last question may be "yes." You may end up with a teacher like this and a feeling that you can do nothing except count the days until his or her retirement. No staff is perfect, but a movie coach is one of those silent and ineffective teachers who can inadvertently influence the culture of expectation among your staff.

The Popular Unteacher

The unteacher is a very tricky species of animal. These folks are wildly popular with students and well liked by their colleagues. They are active club sponsors and participants in extracurricular activities. In general, these creative and charismatic folks are a pleasure to be around and spend a great deal of time at school. At first glance, these folks seem to be the best and brightest that your learning community has to offer.

The challenge, where these teachers are concerned, comes when you take the time to examine the authenticity of what is happening in terms of student learning. Michelle Simmons remembers working with this unteacher:

Oh man, everybody loved Mrs. Tanner. She taught our gifted classes for years. She would have these plays and puppet shows and kids were just clamoring to be in her drama club. I always thought she was a good teacher because the parents respected her so much. Then one day I went to this workshop on authentic learning and I started to really think about the nuts and bolts of classroom instruction. I began wondering about how and why objectives are written for a lesson. I then started to look at Mrs. Tanner differently. I mean, she always had a grand project going on in class. But when I casually asked her why her kids were making a papier-mâché statue or performing a play at the nursing home, she always answered, "Because that is the key to intellectual growth." I realized that this was not an appropriate answer. I also realized that over the years, our ninth-grade English teacher was letting her after-school drama club leak into her activities in the classroom to the detriment of the curriculum.

Essentially, she had effectively moved from English teacher and drama club sponsor to drama teacher. I don't even think she consciously realized this; to her, she was simply being creative.

The finesse required in working with teachers of this kind lies in the necessity of redirecting a teacher's focus with dignity. Again, the appropriate arena to help this teacher reflect on the reality of his or her classroom is the postevaluation conference. Question your unteachers about how their activities are related to standardized grade-level expectations. If they give you an ambiguous answer, avoid bluntly telling them they are wrong. Simply keep asking for a deeper explanation. Remember, these folks think they are doing a great job and their popularity among parents and other constituencies reinforces their self-view. The biggest caveat here for principals is to weigh the political fallout from taking on a teacher like this. If you decide to wrestle with an unteacher, consider his or her political power base. Are you willing to take that on? Is your power base of support strong enough to do so? The odds are that in your rookie year, you are nowhere near ready to overtly challenge a teacher like this because you are the one new to the system and they are one of the power holders sizing you up. Do what you can to build a relationship with this teacher during your first year. Earn this person's trust. Then, in your second year or third year as principal, ask this teacher to be a part of some sort of committee that would allow him or her to learn more about curriculum and instruction. When possible, ask this person what is going on in the committee meetings and use this as a springboard to discuss what authentic teaching and learning is. Invite this teacher to trade classroom observations with another teacher on campus that you believe to be strong in terms of curriculum delivery. Essentially remember these kinds of teachers require your time and patience to help them change their view of what they are doing in the classroom.

He or She Who Does Not Play Well with Others

Instruction is not really the problem with this kind of teacher. The main issue here has to do with collegiality. You will hear about this teacher from other teachers or staff who come to you and complain about this person. This teacher may be a gossip, or passive aggressive, or may just be a mean person. In any case, the first step whenever there is a conflict among staff members is for you to mediate it. Have both parties come to your office and sit them across from you and next to each other. In this situation, you don't have to be so concerned about making sure that the teachers' level of threat is lowered: These folks are in your office because they can't seem to act like grown-ups. Ask both parties what the problem is. Then listen to what both parties have to say. Ask clarifying questions of both parties. Share your view that this issue needs resolution in order to ensure a productive and professional environment for students. Finally, ask what it will take from both parties to resolve this issue. Listen, again. Then reiterate what you heard that both parties are willing to do. End your mediation by informing both teachers that you will be checking with each person individually in a few weeks about the status and climate of the campus since the mediation.

If this is the latest of several mediations that involve one particular person, consider having a frank individual discussion with the teacher who does not play well with others. Start by telling the teacher, "I need your help. Tell me what is going on with you and your colleagues. It appears that there is a pattern of conflict. Every time I am asked to get involved in a conflict, you seem to be a part of it."

Listen to what the teacher has to say, respond appropriately, and then feel free to also share if appropriate, "I understand what you are saying. However, at this point I am concerned enough to let you know that your professional choices may be reflected in the evaluation instrument." If you decide to throw the gauntlet down, make sure you have the documentation and time to actually reflect your concerns in the evaluation. And be prepared for a fight. This type of teacher directs anger toward others and is a bully. Your comments may result in this person finding union representation and possibly filing a grievance. Be warned that tackling a teacher like this is stressful because these people enjoy a fight and stirring up trouble. Your best defense is careful documentation and working closely with your personnel director.

The Sixth Man

The standout characteristic of the sixth man is consistency. These are the professionals who aren't exactly superstars but they form the backbone of your teaching staff. The sixth man doesn't make waves; he doesn't have student discipline problems. The sixth man just does his job and is always on point, ready to produce. These folks make good mentors for younger teachers.

Because these folks are not as high profile as the superstar franchise players, principals overlook their efforts and/or take them for granted. Principals may skip pop-ins to these classrooms in order to devote more time to those teachers who need more attention. Avoid slipping into this poor management behavior. Pop-ins and notes of acknowledgment are the currency that keep these teachers loyal and reinforce to them that they are valued. Don't ignore these people simply because they don't give you any trouble. These teachers are the perfect group to gauge how curriculum adoption is going in the classroom. Seek out these folks to tell you what they think of the new textbook or program that the district has mandated. Empower these folks to also be decision makers on various committees that affect the structure of your school committee. One final consideration is that these classrooms are the most fun to visit. Why? Because when you are in there, you will not have to worry about documenting what you see for a file or conferencing with the teacher later. Go to these classrooms to reconnect with students and enjoy a break from the rigors of your day.

The Franchise Player

These are the rarest of teachers. If you are lucky you will have one, maybe two, on staff. They are respected by their peers, the parents, and members of every level of a school community. They may or may not have a teaching award hanging in their classroom. These people understand their profession to be a calling and regularly seek opportunities to grow intellectually and as leaders. Many times these are also the people who end up transitioning into administrative positions during their career. While this is good for administration, this movement depletes the richness of a school's pool of teachers.

The care and feeding of the franchise player begins with mentoring. Young players need the support of seasoned veterans and they need your individual support. These are the people who will help you implement curriculum and give you insights from a teacher's perspective about various issues. A franchise player is not necessarily young. They can be sages with a ten- or twenty-year career to brag about. Give these people the respect they deserve and do not be afraid to discuss frankly with them your concerns about implementing change and how you see them helping your staff. In addition to administrative roles, these people make great curriculum specialists. Nurture these people by empowering them to be decision makers for your campus, recognizing their efforts in personal notes and visiting in their classes. Think of the classroom of a franchise player as a place where other faculty can visit and observe these teachers in action. Above all, remember to include these teachers in your vision for school reform early on so that they can help lead changes for the rest of your staff.

CHAPTER 4 INSTANT REPLAY:
KNOWING YOUR PLAYERS

1. These categories are only basic general descriptions, they are a thumbnail to help you understand the teachers you are supporting and avoid political pitfalls.
2. Consider the political consequences of your actions toward any of these teachers.
3. Franchise players as well as the sixth man make great mentors for rookies.
4. Explain to your mentors how you want them to work with rookies.
5. Keep up with rookies and mentors through coffee talks, luncheons, and annual meetings.
6. Documentation will help you keep track of concerns you see in the classroom.
7. Encourage your staff to observe each other teaching as a way to highlight your expectations.
8. Do not take the actions of your staff members personally. What they say and do is a reflection of who they are. A big shot will be rude to anyone who is the principal because of their issues with authority.
9. Do not expect to change all of your challenging teachers.
10. Do not expect to be able to get rid of your challenging teachers. Some are challenging in ways that have nothing to do with the evaluation instrument.

5

WHEN THINGS GET UGLY

Howard held his breath as the secretary of the Jackson School Board addressed the audience:

"According to Jackson School District Governing Board Policy JGB14.13, the district administrative staff is seeking board approval for the renewal of the following full-time teaching contracts for these teachers: Antonia Douglass, Mark Kretovics, Stephen Thomas, and Taniesha Holland."

The president of the Jackson Governing Board then asked, "All those in favor signify by saying 'aye.'" Immediately, a unanimous chorus of agreement came from all the board members sitting on the dais.

The secretary continued, "In accordance with Jackson School District Governing Board Policy JGB14.15, the district administrative staff is seeking board approval for the termination of a full-time teaching contract for the following person: Donna Bains."

The president of the Jackson Governing Board repeated, "All those in favor signify by saying 'aye.'" And once again, a unanimous chorus of agreement came from all the board members.

The whole procedure took less than two minutes. Howard got up from his chair at the back of the audience. He walked out of the meeting toward his truck in the parking lot, while the secretary droned on the next agenda item through the microphone. He thought to himself, "They don't even realize that those two minutes were the result of six months of classroom visits, a stupid grievance that wasted hours of my time, and so many hours of documentation I cannot even count them. It happened so fast, I wonder if anyone in the audience realizes that they just watched a teacher being fired."

Howard was a little surprised that Donna Bains was absent from the meeting. He had last talked to her two weeks earlier, in his office at Republic School. At that final meeting with Mrs. Bains, Howard had informed her, in the presence of the director of human resources and the Jackson Teachers' Union representative, that he was submitting paperwork for the termination of her teaching contract to the Jackson governing board.

Mrs. Bains responded to this inevitable news by screaming that the actions being taken against her had nothing to do with her abilities in the classroom but that this was really because Howard was the most racist principal in the district. Howard sat steel-jawed as Donna went on to tell him that she would be informing the NAACP, the ACLU, the WMJ news team, and anyone else who was willing to listen to her story.

Because Mrs. Bains threw down the gauntlet, Howard was expecting a circus at the Jackson governing board meeting where her contract was on the agenda. Despite all the threats, there was no rumbling tonight. But that did not mean it was over for Howard. He fully expected some sort of snapback on his efforts before the week was over.

Beyond the sheer drama of Mrs. Bains's nonrenewal, Howard was bewildered as to why this teacher "just didn't get it." He had put her on three plans of improvement and spent a few thousand dollars of professional development funds for Donna to attend workshops and shadow other teachers. None of that mattered in the teachers' lounge, where Mrs. Bains chose to hold court and put her spin on the whole situation. So now he had a staff in turmoil because he chose to do his job and ensure that quality teachers supported the students in the Republic School community. Howard knew that this is what happened when the principal made the decisions no one wanted to make. Howard was a veteran principal, and he was secure enough to realize that leading a school is not a popularity contest. But no matter how many times he was tempted to ignore Mrs. Bains's completely inadequate teaching and take the easy road, he just couldn't. It wasn't right. He believed in his heart that Donna Bains was not good for his students. The problem was that he could not tell his side of the story to anyone on his campus because, in a personnel matter, things are confidential.

Yes, this teacher had now been successfully terminated, but now his character would be put on trial because of someone playing the race card. It frosted Howard to no end. He had prided himself on working to build unity in his school and hire a more diversified staff. That didn't matter right now because Mrs. Bains was assassinating his character to anyone who would listen. Howard tried to remember that this would fade. He knew that he had a reputation for being anything but a racist. It was the whole point of someone taking a cheap shot because he or she didn't like being held accountable that infuriated Howard. Very few careers in education offered such a perverse dynamic than when a person did what he believed was in the best interest of children, he risked very public trials and embarrassments that had nothing to do with his abilities.

Howard unlocked his red truck and muttered, "No doubt about it. . . . This is going to get ugly."

HOW TO SURVIVE AN UGLY MEETING

Without question, there will be some point in your career as an administrator that you will have to tell someone something that he or she does not want to hear. Breaking bad news can range from informing a staff member about a personal tragedy, such as the death of a loved one, to explaining to an employee that they no longer have a job at your school. In any case, the most important thing to remember is to allow the person who is receiving the news to have the most dignity possible.

Remember to have conversations of this type in private. If you are informing someone of a tragedy, be aware that the more time you spend trying to talk around the news, the more the person listening to you is going to worry and wonder what is going on. However, be tactful; avoid just blurting out the information without letting the person get comfortable. When you have shared what you need to share, listen to that person. Let him or her vent or cry or be angry. Use the listening skills mentioned earlier and remember to be as empathetic as possible. The best support you can give at a moment like this is to allow this person some privacy and deter the interruptions that inevitably happen.

WORKING WITH THE EMPLOYEE WHO IS IN TROUBLE

If the scenario is that you are informing an employee of charges brought against him or her, you will need to talk through a plan of approach with your personnel director, depending on the severity of the charges. Questions for your personnel director include the specifics of the charge, the process to be followed that ensures the preservation of your employee's legal rights, and what the district's expectations are for you in terms of documentation of the meetings you will conduct related to this matter. Finally, don't forget to ask "What happens next?" so that you can understand a timeline and ultimate outcome. Some offenses unfold into a long process that culminates in the termination of an employee. Others unfold into a long process that culminates in a letter being placed in an employee's file.

For example, a student accusing a teacher of sexual harassment is one end of a spectrum, whereas a parent complaining that a teacher is "mean in class" is another. In any case, do not discuss this matter on the sidewalk or during a conversation that takes place while you are on the run. Give this person enough respect to invite him or her into your office at a predetermined time. Be aware that when you extend this invitation, the person will feel more anxious. If your goal is to increase their anxiety, fine. If your goal is to lower your employee's level of threat, then find a time in the day when you can see him or her in a quiet moment and discuss the problem.

DELIVERING THE BAD NEWS

A good way to start any conversation of this nature is to simply say, " I need your help." Then go into the detail of what has happened. You also might want to remind this person that they could (or should) seek advice from a union representative. Ultimately, you control the tone of a conversation and a difficult exchange may turn ugly because of your actions. Be acutely aware of how you are perceived. Any inflection or shortness in your voice will seem more intimidating or insulting to someone who may feel apprehensive about talking to you about work issues. Your positional power plays a huge role in situations like these. In most cases, your employee is already aware that he or she is in some sort of trouble simply because you are asking to see him or her about a work matter.

If during the discussion your employee becomes insolent or rude, do not take these remarks personally; remember to speak slowly and in a calm voice. If he or she gets angry, try to neutralize the situation by using a broken-record mantra. In other words, answer the employee with, "I understand that you are frustrated and angry. However, the point of this meeting today is to inform you that A, B, and C have happened and that my expectations for you are X, Y, and Z." Keep repeating this until things have calmed down. If things do not calm down—stay calm, repeat your mantra, and then begin to bring the meeting to closure.

Do this by asking if there are any more questions. If there are questions, answer them. If the employee starts to escalate, return to the mantra about the purpose of the meeting and your expectations. You can also add, "At this point I believe we are at closure. We will meet again on such and such date to follow up."

THE PLAN OF IMPROVEMENT

Another way to frame an ugly meeting is to go over a plan of improvement. The use of these documents is usually described in great detail in your district's bargaining agreement and in governing board policy. You can introduce the plan of improvement at the beginning of the meeting by explaining that the purpose of the meeting is to discuss this plan and your expectations. Then discuss the plan. Answer any questions your employee may have. Then explain when you would like to meet again to discuss your employee's progress. You will need to give the employee copies of the plan and do not forget to have him or her sign the plan. If the employee refuses to sign it, calmly respond with "OK" and then write in the employee signature line "Employee refuses to sign." Sign your name on the line and then include the date.

Most employees interpret a plan of improvement as a bad thing. In many instances, the opposite is actually true. A plan of improvement helps people understand specifically where they need to focus to improve in their performance. Explain this to your employee at some point during your meeting. By doing this you demonstrate that you have every expectation that this employee will improve and that you are not persecuting him or her. Above all, you are responsible for preserving the dignity of your employees, especially when you are disciplining them.

If you anticipate a particularly ugly meeting, it is a wise idea to invite your secretary or assistant principal to sit in the meeting to take notes. You can explain to those people present that you invited this person in to take notes in order to allow you to better focus on what is happening in the meeting.

If your employee brings a union representative to the meeting, do not panic. He or she has the right to do so and remember that such representatives are there simply to ensure that the employee is treated fairly. If you are surprised to find a union representative present, make sure you contact your personnel director after the meeting to debrief what was said and to strategize what may happen next. It is most important to keep your district office informed of any situations at your school that might involve union leadership.

KEEPING A DOCUMENTATION FILE

It is a very good idea after an ugly meeting to make some notes as to what happened while you were fulfilling your responsibilities as a supervisor. You will want to save these notes in case you need to protect yourself later. It is quite common for disgruntled employees to file lawsuits against their former employers. Be prepared for such a backlash by keeping a documentation file in a place that is not easily accessible and name it inconspicuously such as "Rainy Day File." Principals' personal notes related to personnel matters are subject to subpoena in almost every instance, so be careful to keep concise, legible, and professional records. Do not assume that your office is truly private. It is not. If you choose to keep these notes on a computer, be aware that it is possible for someone to access them, just as they would in an obvious file cabinet. Figure 5.1 is an example of a form that you can replicate and use whenever you have an ugly meeting.

Take a cue from the Kennedy clan of Scotland and observe their motto of "avis la fin." When translated from Latin, the phrase means, "Consider the end." Keeping a file of documentation is really like investing in insurance for yourself. Documenting is a practice, which if observed regularly, will ease the necessary work to discipline employees as well as prove that you acted appropriately in particular situations. Do not limit your documentation to only incidences with employees. Figure 5.2 is a list of red-flag situations that should inspire you to document the event, date, and time. Do not forget the importance of responsibly filing your documentation or informing your personnel director of incidences you find particularly significant.

```
Record of Meeting
Date _____        Time _____

Location of meeting _____

Names of those present
_____
_____

Purpose of Meeting _____
_____

Points discussed _____
_____
_____
_____
_____

Date set of follow-up meeting _____

Purpose of follow-up meeting_____

If appropriate, name(s) of district office personnel contacted after meeting to debrief
_____
```

Figure 5.1. Sample Record of Meeting Form

IF THERE IS A GRIEVANCE

Grievances can be looked at in two ways: Either they are good things that improve the collaboration between employees and supervisors and ensure fair treatment of all, or they are acts of vengeance. Sometimes they can be both. Grievances are also sometimes filed to specifically test a particular district policy. However, in most cases, grievances are filed because someone is angry. The key to dealing with a grievance that is filed

Red Flags That Should Inspire Documentation

- Any heated exchange with an employee, student, or parent
- A visit to a poorly managed classroom
- Tardiness of an employee
- An employee who presents him or herself at work as under the influence of drugs or alcohol
- A visit to a classroom that is full of students unattended by their teacher (who may be down the hall on the phone or copy machine)
- The absence of an employee from their assigned place of supervision during lunch or recess
- A classroom in chaos
- A classroom poorly supervised by a substitute
- A teacher or employee humiliating a student unnecessarily
- An adult behaving in any inappropriately sexual manner
- An employee cursing in front of students
- An employee sexually harassing students or fellow employees
- Emails that threaten legal action or physical harm to you or anyone at your school (print and save the email and your response)
- Phone calls that threaten legal action or physical harm to you or anyone at your school
- Notes that threaten legal action or physical harm to you or anyone at your school
- Visits from detectives or police officers investigating issues on your campus

Figure 5.2. List of Red-Flag Situations

against you is to honestly reflect on the situation surrounding the grievance, then ask yourself if you believe you breeched policy in some way or if you treated an employee unfairly. If you truly believe that your professional choices resulted in the matter that is now grieved, then accept your mistake and go through the process. The principalship is a profession in which *we learn by doing*. Making mistakes is part of the territory. If this is the case, accept the outcome of the grievance process, learn from it, and go on.

If you reflect on the grievance brought against you and believe that you truly have done nothing wrong, take comfort in knowing that you acted appropriately and professionally and talk to your personnel director about what happens next. You also might seek advice from your administrative colleagues as how to best handle the situation.

Once you are notified of a grievance (usually it is in writing and you will find the memo in your box), contact your director of personnel and discuss the issues being grieved and your perception of the politics surrounding the grievance. Now is the time to be honest. If you are not honest with those administrators who will be trying to support you, the consequences down the road will be serious. It is much better to own up to any inappropriate choices you made than to allow your supervisors and support network to be surprised by members of a grievance committee later. It should also be obvious to you not to discuss these issues with employees on your campus. Do not confide in your most trusted teacher about a grievance; eventually these actions will divide a staff.

WHEN TO GET AN ATTORNEY

People usually think of an attorney as the person to help them get out of trouble. In many ways that is true. The problem with this line of thinking is that it often includes the implication that when you retain an attorney *you have done something wrong*. This is not always the case.

Your school district has one or more law firms that represent your district in many instances such as a grievance or a special education arbitration issue. Most of the time, these attorneys will represent you in relation to your actions while in the line of duty to the district. However, there are a few situations in which you may want to seek your own legal counsel. These situations include if you are charged with a crime or if you believe that you are being treated unfairly by your district (i.e., wrongful termination, sexual harassment, discrimination, etc.). The local professional school administrators' association will also have an attorney available to you if you are a member (this is a common benefit for members). The caveat about retaining counsel through these avenues is that the attorney you find may not adequately meet your needs. Or the level of this attorney's expertise may not be to your best benefit.

Because most people rarely work with attorneys, the process of retaining one can be intimidating. Do not be intimidated. Retaining an attorney is very simple. You call them and make an appointment in which you explain all the details of your dilemma. You must be completely honest at this meeting and share everything you think may be related to your situation. The attorney will keep this information confidential and then explain to you what he or she thinks your options are. You have the right to inquire as to what the retainer fee is. In some cases, it is five hundred dollars and in some cases it is more. He or she may allow you some flexibility in terms of when and how you pay the retainer via a payment plan or the like. In both a civil or criminal case against your district, your attorney will undoubtedly ask for a copy of your district's governing board policy manual. Be prepared and get an extra copy when it is issued to you so that you can give him or her one.

RAINY-DAY INSURANCE

Prepare now for a situation in which you may need strong legal counsel by finding out the names of the firms that represent your district. Keep a list of attorneys and their specialties that your district retains. Add to this a list of names of attorneys that could help you should you find yourself in need of legal support. Be smart and politically astute by creating this list before you need it. Contact your school law professor and ask him or her to list the best attorneys in your state. Also ask your school law professor to list the best attorney available who represents school principals in contract or employment disputes. Ask your seasoned colleagues (especially your friends in personnel) about who they have worked with and who they respect. You can simply explain, if your inquiries are met with questions, that you just "wondered how all that stuff worked in our district."

You may never have any bumpy or stressful times in your career. But if you do, you will be that much more prepared by having the list in figure

Attorney References

- The name(s) and phone number of the law firm(s) that represent our district

_____

- Name of attorneys and their specialties (special ed, employee termination, etc) in the above firm(s) _____

_____

_____

- The name, phone number and address of the best legal counsel for school administrators in my state that specialize in principal termination cases

_____

_____

- The name, phone number and address of the best legal counsel for school administrators in my state that specialize in slander/libel cases

_____

_____

- The name, phone number and address of the best legal counsel that specialize in criminal cases _____

_____

- The name, phone number and address of the best legal counsel that specialize in sexual harassment cases _____

_____

- The name, phone number and address of the best legal counsel that specialize in discrimination cases

_____

_____

Figure 5.3.   List of Attorney References

5.3 completed and on hand as a reference for both you and the attorney who represents you.

On a final note concerning legal issues and ugly meetings, here is a list of fifteen scenarios (figure 5.4) that will take your career off track in one way or another. While these may seem outrageous, they are true mistakes that have been made by your colleagues. You may remember some of these by learning about them on the evening news.

WHEN IT IS TIME TO LEAVE

A veteran administrator once said, "Being a principal is kind of like being the knight on the white horse riding into the village to save everyone and fight the bad guys. The problem is, sometimes, in the middle of sword fights, and dodging the flaming arrows, you don't understand that someone has shot your horse and that the poor animal is about to crumble and die beneath you. In terms of the principalship, it can be difficult to realize when it is time to leave."

Fifteen Ways to Make Your Career More Difficult

1. Abusing alcohol in front of your employees
2. Abusing alcohol or drugs at work
3. Earning a DUI citation
4. Hiring, or trying to hire, a prostitute
5. Having an affair with a co-worker
6. Stealing money from the pop machine, PTA money box, or anywhere else
7. Engaging in sexual activity, of any kind, at work
8. Cursing in inappropriate arenas
9. Demeaning your employees through sarcasm
10. Yelling at anyone in public
11. Arriving late to work consistently and leaving early consistently
12. Failing to report when you are informed of suspected sexual abuse of a student
13. Losing your temper regularly at work
14. Consistently lying
15. Failing to meet evaluation paperwork deadlines as outlined in the bargaining agreement

---

Figure 5.4. Fifteen Ways to Make Your Career More Difficult

Leaving is not a bad thing. People often misunderstand the cycle of leadership and organizations. Willard Waller (1938) explained this cycle by saying that by definition, a leader's function is to make decisions. Since every decision made by that leader will anger at least one person, over the course of time the leader will have made enough decisions to anger enough people so that she or he has worn out his or her welcome. Essentially, leaders, like milk and bread, have a shelf life. So how do you know when you are stale?

The first step is to analyze the progression of your principalship. It can be visualized as a bell curve, with the ascension of the curve associated with the honeymoon period and the first effort made by the principal to fit in. Essentially the world is sunshine and roses during this time. Once the principal has achieved "fit," trust and loyalty from different members of the school community follow. It is during this time that the principal reaches his or her peak, in terms of the ability to institute change and foster loyalty among his or her constituencies. The duration of the peak depends on how the principal deals with conflict and if the principal is supported by his or her superintendent.

If the principal has a network of support from members of every constituency, then conflict will be easier to resolve. The principal can also avoid harm by avoiding decisions that make waves in the community. One view of this tactic is that by producing small or no waves rather than big ones, improvements can be made within a system over an extended amount of time. The other view of this tactic is that avoiding decisions is not really leading.

The peak period of effectiveness on the principal's bell curve will eventually drop for one of two reasons:

1. Too many people are angry about changes that are occurring.
2. Too many people are angry because no changes are occurring.

In either case, the principal has become stale and the descending curve shows that he or she no longer "fits." Keep in mind that one can still be liked and no longer fit. An example of this phenomenon is when you hear a teacher say this about a principal,

"Yeah, that Mr. Starr. . . . He's a nice guy and everything. And I sure wouldn't want to hurt his feelings, but I don't think he does anything. I guess we are actually pretty lucky. I mean no one on staff really worries about their evaluation because we know they will be great. I am just not sure I see him as leadership material. It doesn't matter though. He's a nice guy and he lets me do my job."

As a leader, your skin should crawl when you hear something like this. The principalship is not about being liked. Clearly, Mr. Starr is not respected. And clearly he doesn't hold anyone accountable. His staff may be happy, but are they embracing accountability?

Ask yourself the questions outlined below annually to see if your shelf life has expired.

The most important thing to remember is that the principalship is a marathon sport, not a fifty-yard dash. Lots of principals start at one building and move to another. Moving is not a sign of failure. Some principals

---

Am I Still Effective?

1. Do I still command respect among my staff?

2. Do I still fit?

3. What will it take for me to fit again if that is what I want?

4. Am I in the position to choose whether to stay or go?

5. Am I willing to do or say what it takes to fit again?

6. What are the benefits and risks of staying?

7. What are the benefits and risks of leaving?

8. If I don't want to fit here anymore, where do I want to go?

9. What will I need to get me where I want to go?

10. Whose help do I need to get me where I want to go?

11. Do I need a lawyer or legal advice?

(like many CEOs) thrive on going into a building, shaking it up and creating change, and then moving on to facilitate change in another system. These dragon slayers are definitely change makers. The downside for principals is that this is a stressful way to approach leadership.

Other principals prefer to find a system and give their entire professional life to one school community. Both approaches to leadership are equally acceptable. Your job, as a rookie, is to figure out which approach feels best for you.

CHAPTER 5 INSTANT REPLAY:
THE UGLY PART OF LEADERSHIP

1. When delivering bad news to an employee, above all else make efforts to preserve their dignity.
2. If an employee becomes insolent during a meeting, be a broken record.
3. Documentation is a very, very, good thing.
4. Be professional and concise in your documentation.
5. Do not assume that items in your office are completely confidential.
6. Learn your governing board policies as they relate to personnel issues via your personnel director.
7. Regularly inform your personnel director of conflicts at your school and seek his or her input regarding strategy with employee issues.
8. Create and keep on hand a list of attorneys for your reference.
9. Be honest if you are grieved and learn from your mistakes.
10. Pay attention to your shelf life and know when to gracefully move on.

6

TRAINING FOR A CRISIS

North High's school gymnasium was filled to capacity. The crowd was so loud that the bleachers shook. Rob Louis, North's announcer, roared into the microphone,

"That slam dunk gives North a two-point lead with thirty seconds to go to cinch the City Series title." The bleachers on both sides of the court rumbled with stomping feet. The North High cheerleaders were shouting, "De-fense . . . De-fense."

"It's good!" Rob yelled as South High's point guard Marcel Jones passed to Wesley Roberts who shot a fifteen-footer from the baseline. Now the game between the North High Tigers and the South High Cowboys was tied. North's head coach, Kit Laverne, called his final time-out. The fans went ballistic; they were screaming and stomping louder by the minute.

Marco Marinucci, North's athletic director, was standing in the gym doorway to the locker room looking at the crowd. He was struck by the colors the audience was wearing. "If this was another game in a different neighborhood," he thought, "there would be a sea of black and orange Tiger fans on one side and a sea of red and white Cowboy fans on the other. But this is North High School and this crowd isn't here just to see a basketball game. These folks are here in full force to represent their neighborhood, their gangs, and their turf. So instead of school colors, these kids sport powder blue Timberland shoes and the Rocawear jeans of the North Side Boys. Over there are the black FUBU boots and Ecko hoodies of the South Side Posse." This was no ordinary game, even by North's standards. This was simply the latest chapter in the long-standing North side–South side turf war.

Turf issues were of such concern this time around that North's principal, Rolinda Jones, had asked for the police to provide a squad from their urban task force. The six men were in full urban support gear, from their camouflage boots to their bulletproof vests. They had posted themselves not only in the gym but also at different points on campus.

As the crowd jumped to its feet, Marco noticed that the police were now talking on walkie-talkies and holding their earpieces. He looked up in the stands and saw a pocket of bodies near the top of the bleachers swaying like wheat in a field. The wave began to crescendo into a writhing roller coaster. People in lower stands were now turning their attention away from the court and up to the movement above. Marco realized the people were shoving each other and walked quickly across the court. He reached the bottom of the bleachers just in time to hear someone yell "fight!" He climbed up through the chaos, pulling people apart to make a path. He jumped right in the middle of four boys throwing punches at each other. As he was yelling, "Knock it off!" and restraining a student, a member of the urban task force appeared to help escort the troublemakers out of the gym. One of the North Side Boys involved in the fight had a swollen eye and his lip was gushing blood. It was Terrell Higgs, a junior in Marco's math class.

Mr. Marinucci ordered, "Terrell, you go with the sergeant to the front office," and then caught his breath for a second. He looked up to see the game clock was stopped because of the fight. North High's staff was on the court holding ropes in an effort to prevent people from rushing out of the stands and onto the floor. The rhythmic cheering had now changed into the random shouts, curses, and screams of a crowd on the verge of pandemonium. Marco looked to the principal to see what she wanted to do next and thought, "When in the hell did they go over riot control in our crisis workshop?"

THE SCOOP ON CRISIS PLANS

In terms of how our society looks at school safety, there is a one-word historic milestone that defines how we view schools and their vulnerability to a crisis: Columbine. Violence and student vulnerability was something that happened at "other people's schools" before the horrible tragedy happened at the Colorado high school in 1999. Since that event, communities realized that violence can happen at anytime in a school community. Furthermore, the Columbine tragedy served as a wake-up call for school personnel. Educators, as well as parents, began to recognize that student issues centering on self-esteem and a sense of belonging can escalate situations that compromise student safety. In this rush of national concern over how to prevent crisis in a school, administrators, counselors, and teacher groups flocked to review, revamp, and refocus on the ever-present crisis plan.

So what is a crisis plan? Before Columbine, a crisis plan was a few sheets of paper in every school employee's handbook outlining what to do in case of a fire, tornado, power outage, or hurricane. Lockdowns, a procedure in which every teacher locks their door in an effort to keep students safe from a campus intruder, might have been included in a plan. Crisis plans were usually reviewed with the staff every August at the "welcome back" faculty meeting for five minutes.

After Columbine, many communities demanded to know what schools were doing to ensure the safety of their students. How did superintendents respond to this? By whipping out a crisis plan and reviewing it in community meetings of the board of education. The phrase "lock down" became part of the new safety lexicon for room mothers and reporters delivering the dinner-hour news.

As time passed, the whir of information about Columbine High School and teenage angst faded from the national spotlight. Community members again felt sort of safe. Therefore, the discussions about safety faded from the national and local spotlight. There is one horrific problem with the reality described here: The dynamics in a school community that contribute to potentially violent situations have not faded.

Interest groups, particularly school counselors and those who specialize in student and community social issues, continue to share with those who will listen that not enough is being done to prevent violence in schools. Why? Because they are the sporadic events that fall into Johari's Area of Unknown Activity (Luft, 1970). We are still stuck with not really knowing what to do, except to learn from our experience. Furthermore, it is difficult for our culture to put money and resources into events that we cannot predict. Like all politicians, school leaders have this impossible gray line to walk with their communities: Too much talk about violence prevention and you are viewed as an alarmist, wasting funding on "feel good" counseling activities for kids and teachers instead of academic necessities. Conversely, if you fail to give enough attention to violence prevention, you are vulnerable and unprepared for particular situations.

The rest of this chapter is dedicated to considering various issues surrounding crisis management from the perspective of the new principal— not from the sanitized and politically appropriate perspective of the published governing board crisis plan on the shelf by the copy machine. The bottom line is that where crises are concerned there are two realities, the one surrounding questions that your district answers and the other reality surrounding the questions that your district cannot (or will not) answer.

WHAT IS MY ROLE?

The hard thing about being the principal is that in many cases you are responsible for deciding what sort of role you will play in a crisis, regardless of what parameters your district provides to you. Take, for example, the story of Mr. Johnny Chavez, a principal in Phoenix, Arizona:

> Right after Columbine, our district's administrative team had a meeting to discuss school safety. We went over the crisis plan, and talked about how to help our students feel safe at school. And then the question came up of "What do we do if we hear that there is a person on campus with a gun?" One of my colleagues who was a principal said that she believed that the best course of action was for her to stay in her office, call a lockdown, call the police, and wait for them to arrive to take care of the situation. Another one of my principal colleagues said that she absolutely disagreed. She believed that calling the police was appropriate, and so was the lock-down. But there was no way she was going to stay in her office while there was a chance that there was a person on campus posing a serious threat to her students. I agreed with her. The teachers are not really responsible for disarming or dealing with the bad guys. Frankly, I see that as part of my job. In some instances, I am the campus cop. And, yes, the police need to hurry up and get to my school to help—but I am not going to sit around when I could be doing something to help ensure a safe and orderly environment for my kids. That's part of being a leader, isn't it? By definition I need to lead with heart. My community depends on it. And having heart in my book also means having some courage. Of course what I believe does not have to be the same as what anyone else believes. And that is one of the important nuances of leadership.

You need to decide on which end of the spectrum you fall in terms of sacrificing your personal safety. You may be told endless times that your job is not to be the law enforcement office on your campus. And you are absolutely not paid to risk your life as police officers do.

However, you may encounter a situation where the police are on their way to your campus to respond to a call concerning a weapon, *and you are the one dealing with the weapon and the person who is holding it.* Now what are your supposed to do? Are you willing to risk your own personal safety? Maybe you feel that you will have no choice, as Mr. Chavez did. Of course it is essential to recognize that no principal's contract specifies that the school administrator is expected to risk his or her own safety. Wherever your personal beliefs fall concerning the risks you are willing to take in order to ensure a safe and orderly environment, make sure you have a plan that you have specifically discussed with your superintendent that outlines who will do what on your campus in terms of crisis intervention. Furthermore, if you have never taken a class on gun safety, consider enrolling in these short and important seminars as one more way to prepare yourself for unexpected situations.

Another way to think ahead is to consider the questions listed below.

Stuff to Think about Before (and If) I Am the Hero

a. Does my secretary and the district office have current emergency contact phone numbers for all of our employees and are they updated regularly?

b. Have I taken a self-defense class?

c. Have I participated in a discussion with my principal colleagues, the local police precinct, and the superintendent as to what the specific expectations are concerning my role and weapons on campus?

d. If I work alone and at odd hours in my office (late at night or on weekends), do I practice behaviors that ensure my safety?

e. Have I discussed the challenges of my position in terms of crisis management with my family?

f. Is my home phone number and address public knowledge?

THE RECIPE FOR A CRISIS PLAN

When you review your district's crisis plan, odds are that you will notice the plan to be painfully detailed in some areas and painfully lacking details in others. The places that lack details are where you need to start making lists of questions for yourself. These questions should be the basis of a conversation with your superintendent and other colleagues. Consider these questions to help get your brain warmed up.

Brainstorming Questions for the District Crisis Plan

1. Is there a phone tree of district personnel and an understanding of whom to call and when?

2. Is there a phone tree of campus personnel and an understanding of whom to call and when?

3. Is there a list of personnel who will serve as counselors for students and staff during the days after the crisis?

4. Is there a calendar that outlines in-service dates for the above listed staff so that each employee understands what the expectations are during a crisis?

5. Does the district adhere to this calendar?

6. Are you and other administrators briefed as to how to talk to the press?

7. Does the plan cover a range of crises from the unusual, such as a mercury spill, to the more expected, such as a fire or power outage?

8. Does your staff carry and use two-way radios? If so, does that include one for the custodian and the nurse?

9. Do you practice regular lockdowns along with fire drills on your campus?

10. Has your staff been briefed as to how to handle the media in a postcrisis situation?

11. Has your staff been briefed as to how to support students after and during a crisis?

12. Do your secretaries and office staff know what to do in case a threat is called into the school? Is there a list of questions to ask the person calling posted near their phone?

THE CULTURE OF PREVENTION

The secret to dealing with a crisis lies in what you have done before the *crisis happens.* Being prepared is more than a crisis plan and in-service or two that helps everyone understand what to do in the midst of a campus drama. The first most basic focus for your administrative team is to build relationships with students. You and your counselors and assistant principals need to be out on campus and be seen—every day. Being out and about also means that you need to invest in talking with students while you are out. Employees at every level should be encouraged to invest time in talking with the kids, even the janitor, when they can. These efforts at relationship building assure two things:

1. that students are more likely to confide in an adult staff member when they hear through the grapevine about a threat to their learning environment,
2. that when you or another administrator enters a classroom with the purpose of investigating reports of a student having a weapon in his or her possession, it is not as disruptive as if you are never in the classroom.

To further explore point 2, consider this story from Nancy Ari, a middle school principal responsible for a 1300-student school in the heart of warring gang territory in a large city in the western United States:

There were three big gangs that claimed members of our student body. Because our seventh- and eighth-grade middle school is the largest in our district we had lots of challenges, the greatest challenge being at dismissal time. You see, the older brothers and sisters of our students who were gang members would pull up in our parking lot or next to the sidewalk when the final bell rang and would grab a student who was the younger sibling of a member of an opposing gang and take them away and beat him or her up. The purpose was to scare the sibling and tell the gang member that his or her family was not safe. We beefed up our security at dismissal. We started doing peer mediations; we had three resource officers at our school and coordinated police support at neighboring high schools and in the community. We even called in the gang task force unit. And luckily, these types of incidences only happened three times in a school year. The fear this created among students was unbelievable. And as you might expect, the rumor mill was in full gear. It seemed that every time I turned around, another student had reported to a staff member that so-and-so was carrying a gun, knife, or a machete.

All those reports had to be investigated, which meant interrupting a class: The interruptions meant stirring the rumor mill every time you asked to see a student with his or her backpack outside the classroom. In an effort to stop the drama, our team decided to make sure that, for every time we asked to see a student for an investigative reason, we also would visit a classroom and pull a student out to give them some kudos. Eventually, teachers and kids just realized that we were in classrooms and wanted to see students for all sorts of reasons, not just because there was something dramatic going on. Everything calmed down after a while, but our team decided to still make a point of pulling kids out for various reasons to ensure that this practice became part of our culture. It is kind of like fire drills, you know? Every time you have one, you have to nag everyone out of the building because they are shuffling along. Why? Because teachers and students always think it is just a drill. In many ways, this is a good thing, so that if a fire happens, no one panics. They are leaving the building thinking that it is just a drill.

In terms of considering point 1, it is important to remember that creating a culture of prevention rests on the efforts of everyone on your staff. You will need to put efforts into educating your community as well. One was to approach this issue to have a school theme. You could even use the previously mentioned theme of embracing accountability. What this means for students is the understanding that they are responsible and accountable for a safe and orderly environment in their school, even if they do not bring weapons. You need to help your staff understand how to teach their students to report rumors of threats to campus safety and any other related information to an adult whom they trust. These conversations with students should be meaningful and rest on the lesson that all students are responsible for maintaining a safe and orderly environment. Refusing to tattle on a friend who is bragging about a weapon is just as irresponsible as having the weapon itself.

When students are in an environment where they feel comfortable in sharing information such as this, they are more likely to share their concerns with a staff member. Again, even the prevention of student safety comes back to the importance of building and maintaining relationships between teachers, students, and staff.

Another very helpful idea to encourage student reporting of violence or other concerns is to establish a "tip line" at your school. Several phone companies are willing to set up a phone number that students can call twenty-four hours a day and leave anonymous messages relaying their concerns about campus issues. Talk to you district facilities manager and then set one of these up with your local phone company. Then amplify your initial dissemination of tip line publicity with posters and flyers sent home about how students can use it to report any concern they have about any safety issues related to school. Call the reporter who covers the school beat at your local paper and ask to give an interview about this for a story.

When you establish this tip line, it is imperative that you check it daily and follow up on any calls you receive. The concept of reporting anonymously will not work if the word gets out to the community that no one ever does anything with the reported concerns. When you are able to alleviate a situation, such as a theft, threat, or report of impending fight, celebrate the success in the regular newsletter home to parents. That way, your community knows how effective your idea is and other students will be encouraged to use the tip line.

THE CRISIS TEAM

Another facet of preparation is the development of your crisis team. Your district plan will undoubtedly describe your school's crisis team as a group of people who may or may not include counselors, school nurse, psychologist, administrators, maintenance staff, secretarial staff, and various teachers on special assignment who are not directly tied to a classroom (i.e., the literacy specialist or librarian).

The idea behind a crisis team is that it is a group of people at all tiers of a school organization who are mobile on campus and can coordinate specifics of crisis management. Each member's role is something that should be explored by the team as a whole and made clear to everyone on staff. You should have at least two extended meetings or training sessions a year with your crisis team to talk about strategy and the state of your campus. Your team should also be able to help answer questions about crisis management raised by staff members. You also need to decide how to activate the team. Will you use a code word over the loudspeaker? If that code word is uttered, will all members know to meet at a designated area for briefing or will they simply turn immediately to their assigned task? Make sure details like this are clear to everyone on staff and have regular drills so that all remember what it means when they hear, "Mrs. Gramuffle, please come to the office" on the loudspeaker. Take the time to talk to your principal colleagues in other districts, as well as your own, to learn how they facilitate crisis teams. You will probably be surprised to learn that many of your colleagues do not see this as a priority, because there has not really been a need for one at their school. Do not be lulled into this same mind-set. Effective crisis teams consist of members who understand the importance of their role and who regularly participate in campuswide discussions about campus safety. Ineffective crisis teams are made up of folks who know their name is on a list but are not sure what they are supposed to do during crunch time.

CLASSROOM DISCIPLINE

The bottom line concerning a school's safe and orderly environment rests on each of your teacher's abilities to manage a classroom effectively. If your teachers do not understand your expectations concerning classroom management, or worse yet, if they do not feel accountable for maintaining classroom order, you are leading a school that is begging for some sort of chaotic drama. Your top priority should be a safe school. Yes, it is important that your students learn, but your school needs to be safe. Do not kid yourself if you work in a school that is not in the urban copy of a big city but is located in happy suburbia. Classrooms in chaos happen everywhere because they are managed by incompetent or uncaring teachers. The best way to help your staff understand that you are serious about student safety is to hold teachers accountable by way of the evaluation instrument. When it is reported to you that there are incidences of student violence or disorder in a particular classroom, save the documentation. Use this documentation to put the teacher on a plan of improvement (see the previous chapters for details on plans of improvement).

Make a point to learn about new programs and new classroom management techniques. Then invite your staff to take the same training. NO, not everyone will participate, but the point is to get the word out that you take a well-organized classroom seriously. Volunteer to teach in classrooms regularly; this allows you to figure out what kind of chaos really exists in a class. And above all, do everything you can to maintain your students' dignity.

Take advantage of your school counselor, social worker, resource officer, and psychologist. Ask them to pay attention to workshop opportunities that they find relevant and pass them on to you. Ask these folks to speak to your faculty at meetings in order to give information about issues of concern that range from student suicide predictors, to extinguishing inappropriate student behaviors with dignity, to identifying signs of child abuse. Consider developing a series of courses for students in peer mediation, anger management, and communication/social skills that can be taken as an elective or that are infused in other courses such as health science or human development. Another idea is to consider the use of an alternative school or flex scheduled school for students who might benefit academically and socially from smaller classes and individual attention from their teachers. And finally, book talks about these issues for staff and parents are also a wise investment (for book suggestions, see chapter 11).

ABOUT GANG CULTURE

The 2000 edition of *The American Heritage Dictionary* defines a gang as:

1. A group of criminals or hoodlums who band together for mutual protection and profit. **2.** A group of adolescents who band together, especially a group of delinquents.

What is interesting about these definitions is that the first implies illegal activities involved and the second only hints at illegal activities based on the word *delinquent*. This is essentially how the world of gangs in schools is defined as well. There are true gang members who have criminal records who may or may not be students. These people are often surrounded by other teenagers who have yet to pose any real threat to your school community. Those who have not actually committed crimes may have acted out in other ways that range from fighting (in and outside of the school day) to threats and throwing gang signs.

And then there are those kids who are not really in gangs but wear the same clothing as known gangs in their area and throw (or flash, or show) gang signs to their friends or when they are posing for photographs. Sometimes these teenagers are emulating what they have seen in a music video and sometimes they are not. As we all know, adolescence is the time of drama and posturing. The effective leader understands that the school safety standard concerned revolves around incidents that are disruptive to the educational environment. It can be easily argued that throwing gang signs on campus is a disruption. And this should not be tolerated. The irony is that students are more savvy than ever before and there are many educators who do not even realize the subculture that exists in their schools in this area. Take, for example, the reflections of Gloria Sanders, a high school principal, who, during a professional conference, visited a sister school in Miami, Florida:

> I was really interested in doing some student cultural exchanges with a school similar to mine about three years ago. So I arranged to visit an inner-city school with the same demographics as mine during one afternoon. This public school was interesting to me because it was run by a woman about my age and they had implemented a mandatory school uniform for students. I walked the halls of this fifty-year-old building completely impressed with how every single student was in uniform and that none of the white uniform pants and skirts were dirty. These inner-city kids all had shined shoes and pressed clothes. They all just looked great. While the principal was touring me around, I asked if I could take pictures and she obliged me. As we were talking about student discipline, she shared that there was a zero tolerance for fights at her school. She said occasionally there was a fight but that it was dealt with swiftly. I then watched her take a student to task because his shoelaces were untied. It was very clear that this principal had a formal style and that she was not a woman to be disrespected in any way. What shocked me was that every time I took a picture of a class, the students would pose with their classmates or their teacher and throw the familiar gang sign of a "W" with their left hands on their right arms or an "O" with their left hands by their shoulders. The principal hosting my tour was watching the kids as their pictures were being taken. I must have snapped pictures of at least fifteen classrooms and

in every room there was at least one student throwing a sign. I asked the principal while we were walking around if there was a problem with gangs at her school and she told me "No, we don't have any gangs here."

At one point the principal had to take a call and left me alone with a class. When I saw another gang sign, I was so mad, I just pulled the student aside and said quietly, "Why do you disrespect a visitor to your school by throwing a sign? Don't you think I know what you are doing?" This boy's eyes got huge and at the same moment the principal came back. I decided to leave it at that and walked away. I think the kid was shocked that I had a clue as to what was going on. It bothers me that this principal, who prided herself on students having such a presentable and neat appearance, had no idea that her school had a subculture of students claiming and bragging about the gangs that they belonged to.

The lesson of Gloria's story is to be observant of the details of your school's student culture. Invite a gang task force member to tour your school with you while he or she is out of uniform. Ask for feedback in terms of any symbols or gang signs that he or she observed in your school. Have the gang task force member present his or her insights into identifying gang signs to your staff. If you decide to include in your school policy a rule that forbids gang behavior, make sure your teachers know what gang behavior is and that they enforce the regulation. As Gloria's story illustrates, neat school uniforms don't always equal a school free of underlying conflict.

Another important yet mundane classroom task many teachers ignore is the act of taking role. Oftentimes, a student skips class and is not caught because there is a glitch in the student attendance reporting system in your school. What is more frightening is the thought that a student *is taken* from campus and because a teacher fails to take role or a clerk fails to catch a glitch in the attendance procedures, the student is in danger.

Make sure your office staff understands and follows the practice of checking who is allowed to take whom out of your school. A typical maneuver for a noncustodial parent involved in heated custody battles is to take his or her child out of school and then leave the community. The school secretary or clerk may simply release a child because he or she is told that the person picking the child up is the parent. Encourage your staff to ask for identification, to make a photocopy of this identification, and to have the person there to pick the child up sign in. Write in your school newsletter to parents that, if there is a problem about custody concerning their child or if there are specifics that the staff needs to know concerning who may pick their child up from school, that they need to notify your attendance clerk or the principal. Have your staff check the registration card of every child that an adult comes to get before they release the student. If the student's card has a red marker on the top left corner (for example), this can serve as a red flag to warn staff to be careful concerning authorized adults to pick up that student.

Furthermore, spend some time considering the ease of access at your campus. In order to do this, review the questions below:

Campus Access Inventory

1. How many entrances are there to my campus?

2. Is there an ability to gate these entrances and control the flow of visitors during the school day?

3. Are there holes in the campus fencing or spaces on the campus that are not fenced and therefore easy for intruders to pass through?

4. Has our staff decided to mandate that all visitors must check into the administrative office?

5. If we have mandated an office check in, do we enforce it?

6. Are staff members required to wear an ID badge?

7. Are visitors required to wear an ID badge?

8. If a staff member sees an adult that is unfamiliar to them, would he know to contact the administrative office for follow-up?

9. Are substitute teachers issued ID badges?

10. Is there a sign that explains to visitors that they need to check into the office before walking on the rest of campus?

11. If the staff is required to wear ID badges, do you wear one? (You should, if you are not; you are not above practice and policy.)

12. Are students taught to report any unfamiliar visitors to their teachers or other staff members?

MANAGING CAMPUS EVENTS

Another arena that invites crisis is the campus event. This activity can range from the basketball game described at the beginning of this chapter to a school play, graduation ceremony, prom, or carnival. When you are in the planning stages of such an event, consider the areas of entrance and the process used to determine who belongs where. Use these questions as a guideline for discussions with your planning staff.

Safety Questions for Event Planning

1. Has the equipment (chairs, bleachers, etc.) used in the event been checked for proper functioning?

2. Do students understand that their behavior in school (or lack of it) may cost them the right to participate in this event?

3. Have parents been informed of number 2?

4. Do all staff members supervising this event know who to inform if they see something suspicious?

5. Have police been contacted to provide extra support?

6. Who is supervising the flow of traffic and parking?

7. Is there water available for people if needed?

8. Have you decided when it is acceptable for you to leave the site after the event is over?

9. Have you made efforts to inform the families in your campus neighborhood of the upcoming event and the inconvenience it may cause in terms of parking and traveling up and down the street?

10. Have you had discussions with the staff working the event about crowd control?

11. Have you had discussions with your staff as to what to do with a person or student at the event who is under the influence of alcohol or other substances?

THE WALK-THROUGH

On a construction site, the foreman will walk through the entire site on a regular basis to look at what is going well, what is happening that is challenging, and what safety issues are a concern for all working at the

---

Questions for a Campus Walk-Through

1. What is in disrepair on this site that could cause an injury (a ripped garbage can, broken sidewalk, etc.)?

2. Are there sections of campus that are abandoned during the school day where students could "hang out" instead of attending class?

3. Are there unattractive nuisances such as low roofs and rolled fencing that could invite students to harm themselves on?

4. Are foot traffic patterns marked throughout campus with appropriate signs?

5. Is it clear where offices are?

6. Are rooms and closets locked?

7. Are the rest rooms maintained and cleaned?

8. Are there broken windows that need repairing?

9. Are field houses or other remote storage areas locked and maintained for safety?

10. Is the parking lot paint still visible and is the blacktop still in acceptable condition?

11. Have the bushes, trees, and grass been cut and trimmed appropriately?

12. Are chemicals, such as paint and solvent, out of the reach of students?

13. Are there puddle or ice slicks in spots that could cause injury?

Figure 6.1. Questions for a Campus Walk-Through

site. Principals should take a cue from this practice. To help think about what you are looking at when you walk through your campus, read the questions in figure 6.1.

Finally, after a crisis has passed, have a meeting with your crisis team to discuss what went wrong, what worked well, and what can be learned for the future. Take notes and keep a running log of these pieces of wisdom to add to your August in-service activities for your staff. Use the questions in figure 6.2 to help facilitate a discussion.

The After Crisis Worksheet

1.   What went wrong?

2.   What went right?

3.   Could this have been prevented?

4.   Who should get specific kudos and how will we recognize that person?

5.   What do we want to do differently next time?

6.   What have we learned?

Figure 6.2.   The After Crisis Worksheet

CHAPTER 6 INSTANT REPLAY: TRAINING FOR A CRISIS

1. Know your district's crisis plan.
2. Discuss realistic expectations for maintaining a safe and orderly environment with your superintendent.
3. Train and remind your staff regularly about crisis prevention.
4. Invest in walkie-talkies for your administrative staff, nurse, janitor, and secretary.
5. Set and consistently keep expectations for your staff in terms of classroom management.
6. Use police, social workers, counselors, and your school psychologist as a resource for staff development opportunities.
7. Stay current with the trends in management via journals and professional development conferences.
8. Bring your staff to crisis management workshops.
9. When a crisis is over, debrief with your team and use the information you found for enhancing staff development.
10. Do not assume that crises only happen in other communities.

7

BRINGING THE COMMUNITY TO CENTER COURT

"Hello. . . . Is this Georgia Smith? This is Nancy Hanson, I'm Holly's mother. Our daughters are in the same homeroom. I am calling you because today the nurse sent Holly home in the middle of second period because she wore a skort to school. You know the only reason Holly was in the nurse's office is that she skinned her knee and needed a bandage. That rude nurse said my Holly's outfit was not in compliance with the dress code. And I am just furious . . ."

Georgia Smith, the president of Hess Elementary School's PTA, pulled her car over to the side of the road and shook her cell phone. "Nancy? I'm sorry I think I was in a bad area for this phone. I can hear you better now. Did you say that your daughter was sent home because she wore shorts?"

"No," Nancy replied. "I said she was sent home by that stupid nurse because she was wearing a *skort*. You know those cute little things that look like a skirt in the front and shorts in the back? Well, Holly has a relay race today and she is going to sing in the assembly. These were just so cute and they are navy blue just like the dress code specifies. I thought they would fit the bill. I can never get the girl to wear a skirt and it is going to be so hot and there is no air conditioning in that dreadful building."

"Ahhh yes, a *skort*. Now I know what you are talking about. My daughter wants one of those too. Every time I turn around she is begging me to take her to the mall and buy her a pink one. Now Nancy, you know the principal sent the letter home last August that outlined the new dress code and I know shorts are not allowed."

"Yes, Georgia, I know that, but nothing has been written in the policy about a *skort*. I know because I checked. Furthermore, I have had it with the administration. I tried to talk to the nurse and all she did was argue. I left three messages this week to ask the principal about the skort before Holly wore it this morning, and he never called me back. I even stopped in the office this morning when I brought Holly back to campus in acceptable clothes, and the big chief was in a meeting. I never am able to speak to that principal. You know, my tax dollars pay his salary and I am sick and tired of being ignored."

"I understand your frustration," Georgia said.

Nancy fired back, "Honestly, did we really even have a say in the dress code? I was all for it when Principal Sanders talked about it last April. But I understood that we would have a say as to what was acceptable. It seems like as soon as the parents said, 'OK' the staff decided all by themselves what was going to be acceptable. The next thing I know, there is a long letter two weeks before schools starts in August, explaining what my child was not allowed to wear. Don't these people understand that we mothers spend all of July and most of August looking for school clothes? Sending these rules to me at the last minute after I have spent good money on clothes is irresponsible. This whole thing is just ridiculous; my child is a great athlete and student. She should not be punished because somebody else has taken it upon themselves to interpret a dress code policy that is not clear. I am sick of it."

"You know Nancy; you are not the first person who has come to me with a frustration about the dress code. People are frustrated because the rules are unclear and they are frustrated about how this policy was created without their input. I, myself, have tried to talk to the administration about it and usually I leave the office feeling placated and brushed off. I think it's time we come together as a community and talk about the patterns we have seen with this principal. I am going to host a meeting tomorrow night at my house so that concerned parents can talk openly and in a comfortable environment. Would you come and bring anyone else that you think would be interested in this discussion?"

"Georgia, I know all sorts of mothers who have had it with being left out of the loop. It will be my pleasure to bring them. And, frankly, I think it is time we speak to the school board about this."

WHY COMMUNITY INVOLVEMENT IS SO IMPORTANT

The above story is a perfect example of how a series of little things and miscommunications can evolve into a disgruntled and vocal faction of the community. The frustration Mrs. Hanson feels about the dress code is the symptom of a much bigger problem. Many times principals and other school officials will truncate the decision-making process in the name of efficiency. The motives for this are not always rooted in dictatorship. For example, Jill Allison, a city manager in northeastern Ohio, recalls her experience as part of a school restructuring team:

> I was invited to become a member of a management and vision development team for my daughter's high school. The school district was restructuring itself and our team was responsible for designing a new school in terms of structure, curriculum delivery, culture, and everything

else. Essentially our job was to create a whole new school community. Our group had a facilitator that the district had hired as a consultant. I noticed that the principal was part of the team but did not lead the discussion. Other members of this team were teachers, support staff, community members, and other parents. We had chosen a name for the school and one member had even written a school song. It was really moving. When we heard the song, I got chills thinking about the graduations where that song would be played and the generations of students who would feel the impact of our decisions.

One day at a meeting the facilitator walked in and, in her usual fashion, told us we were doing a great job and that she was so excited to work with us. Then she said that the goal for our two-hour morning session was to decide how the school would be governed. I thought to myself, "Huh? Isn't that what the superintendent and governing board do? What about all those policies? How is that related to our assignment and the new school?" I knew I wasn't the only one wondering, because then a teacher on the team asked about what the governing board bargaining agreement had to do with this and if these decisions were in line with district policies. Then we ended up in a discussion about what campuses teachers would move to and the procedures for people to transfer and who would be allowed to attend the school. No one really had an answer. Every time complicated questions came up, the facilitator would say, "Well now, that is something for the district to decide later. Let's just focus on our school here."

Finally, one of the team members started wondering how teachers would be given the responsibilities of leadership but not the burden of school personnel issues. The facilitator interrupted again and said, "You know we are really short on time, we have ten more minutes and then we need to put this to bed and move on to the next agenda item for today."

I was so irritated with this facilitator. I did not trust her; I did not think she even knew what was going on. Did she think I was stupid? First of all, how can we possibly decide how a school is governed in two hours? And, frankly, I am not sure I was qualified or informed enough to make those sorts of decisions. It all felt like a scam to me. I wondered if we were just being put through the motions and that someone else already knew what they were going to do with this new school. All of this just seemed like a farce, so that someone could say that the community was part of the planning. Worse yet, I worried for a brief moment that nobody had an idea of what was going on and the district was sort of doing this by the seat of their pants and hurrying to meet someone else's timeline. Either way, my confidence in the leadership of the district was dwindling.

Jill's account illustrates the many different factors that play into the decision-making process. Community involvement at a tertiary level does not accomplish the team-building goals of enhancing the credibility of a learning community. As demonstrated in this account, a half-hearted and unorganized involvement can create a lack of trust from community members. However, a thorough and complete effort to include the community facilitates trusting relationships, political support, and resources for the direction a school chooses to follow.

CREATING VEHICLES FOR COMMUNITY INVOLVEMENT

There are many models in the world of leadership that outline specifics for an approach to shared decision making. This approach to leadership comes from a model very popular in industry in which workers have a say in how their organization is run. The idea behind this approach is that because a person has a say in how his or her organization or school is operated, he or she will be more vested in assuring a successful product. Of course, schools are not factories and children are not products. However, experts have reminded practitioners over the last twenty years that the common thread found in effective schools is a core of people who represent all levels of a school community that participate in a shared decision-making process. Other names for models of this ilk include Results-Based Decision Making (Schmoker, 2004); Distributive Leadership (Elmore, 1999); or Learning Communities (Sergiovanni, 1992).

In order to effectively create your team, seek first the council of your principal colleagues. They will be able to tell you what leadership guru's model your district follows. Then make a point to read that guru's book. Before you can create your own team, you need to understand the nuts and bolts of the model observed by your district. Make a point to talk to your principal colleagues about what they have found effective in this model and what they have had trouble with.

For many schools, one sticking point is the difficultly of finding parents and community members who are able and willing to contribute their time to a shared decision-making team. Unfortunately, what can happen if you are not careful is that you have a team with the same members on it every year. When this happens, some other faction of your community or staff may not be represented, and the decisions may not be fair to all of your community.

Ease the comfort level of possible participants by hosting meetings at a time that is convenient for them (in the evening or on weekend mornings). Have meetings directly before or after a school concert, in order to draw parents who would be at the school anyway to see their child. Consider providing transportation to and from the meeting or holding the meeting in the community rather than on the campus grounds. Provide baby-sitting services; or if you have candidates for team membership who do not speak English, provide a translator.

While these efforts are inconvenient for you, they will ensure that your decision-making team is truly representative of the community that you serve. Do not let the convenience of an unbalanced team lure you into allowing this unfair practice to take place.

Members of your team should include teachers, parents, support staff personnel, business leaders, and a student or two. Functioning teams should number between eight and fifteen members. Teams with great numbers in their membership are difficult to facilitate. Strive to host regular meetings and remember to begin and end promptly.

WHAT DOES A TEAM TALK ABOUT?

Creating decision-making teams that include the community but that make no real decisions will quickly backfire. No one appreciates participating in meetings for the sake of saying that there was a meeting. Before the school year starts, brainstorm a list of issues that are important to you. Then analyze the list to see what falls within your realm of responsibility and what could be brought before a team of stakeholders. (To read about how to work with these stakeholders and move your own agenda through, see chapter 8, The Change Game.) Add to the list during the year when scenarios bring to your attention things worth discussing as a whole community. In general, there are three global types of issues that community decision-making teams focus on: School improvement issues, problem solving, and resource attraction.

School Improvement Issues

School improvement issues center around suggestions to make the school a more effective and efficient learning experience for students. Agenda items in this realm for your team may be as mundane as regular reports on the condition of zones and equipment on campus to discussions as to how the parking lot may be reconfigured to provide better traffic flow.

Playground and field areas are an excellent topic for discussions about improvement. Ask your team members what they like and what they don't. Is the equipment that is permanently installed on campus still in working condition? Is it still safe for your students? In the winter months, are there areas that need to be maintained in a different way in order to preserve safety? Should you increase the number of drinking fountains? This author knows of one shared decision-making team at a year-round elementary school in Arizona that opted to raise enough money to install misters at the campus bus boarding area, because there was a concern for student safety in the hot summer and spring months.

Also, consider inviting your maintenance personnel to talk to your team about the issues that are relevant to school safety or site improvement. Perhaps the mats covering the walls in the gymnasium are too old and need to be replaced. Or maybe a member of your student government organization could present ideas for a mural in the library.

School improvement also covers the realm of practices and school policies related to the student body. Revisions or questions about student dress code, discipline policies, and extracurricular policies should be discussed in this forum. Consider student health issues as well. Would your community benefit from a newsletter from the nurse three times a year that has suggestions for keeping the students healthy? Should your school create a welcome center for families new to your school that allows them to register smoothly and acculturate in an environment free from the chaos of the administrative office? These sorts of social and health issues that arise during the school day are the most important discussion topics.

Curriculum is another area that falls within the category of school improvement. Curriculum encompasses much more than simply what is taught in the classroom. In layman's terms, curriculum is essentially everything that happens during the school day. Even recess is considered part of a school's curriculum. The artistry of leadership required when considering the management of curriculum in a school focuses on curricular decisions that cover a broad spectrum of influence and as such it is appropriate to involve different parts of the school community at different junctures. In other words, there is a time and place for those folks who have been trained in such matters to have a say and there is also a time and place for parents, families, and administration to have a say.

Does that mean that all of the decision-making power should go strictly to one of these constituencies? Absolutely not. If the principal is the one person making all the decisions and everyone else is following along, then you have a dictatorship. If a community faction yields such pressure that their views are followed, there is a risk of not serving all the needs of all the students in your school. If teachers are the primary decision makers, then there is a risk that your school is utilizing programs that are only convenient and may not challenge them professionally.

The most important aspect of your job, where curriculum is concerned, is the ability to master shuttle diplomacy. Consider Alex Davis's story as an example of how one uses this approach to bring different factions to consensus:

> I am the principal of a K-8 school whose attendance boundaries shifted three years ago. Before that shift, our student population was primarily Anglo, English-speaking students. After the shift, we had over 50 percent of our students whose primary language is Spanish. It has been a difficult transition to say the least. I hired as many bilingual teachers as I was able to. But the staff did not embrace our new student population completely. The majority of the old guard felt that it should not be their responsibility to teach children who cannot speak English. There were not enough Spanish-speaking teachers to place all the Spanish-speaking students just in their classrooms. And frankly, I felt that is was just morally wrong to segregate our school.
>
> Our district received a large federal grant to implement a schoolwide dual-language acquisition program. Basically, what it would mean for our school is that English-speaking teachers would team teach with Spanish-speaking teachers and all the children would be in classes together. Even-

tually the children would become language brokers for each other. I even heard in a presentation at a district meeting that the best outcome is that students eventually become bilingual. It seemed like a great idea to me. Our English-speaking kids would learn to speak Spanish and our Spanish-speaking kids would learn to speak English.

The district wanted our school to implement this program, and I thought it was the right thing to do. Not everyone in our school agreed. Many of our teachers could be heard saying things such as, "I am not paid to teach those kids." Our parent community was divided. Many thought the idea was wonderful. And others felt that "those kids who can't speak English" interfered with their own child's learning. I was so disturbed at the thought of a segregated school, I plunged ahead.

I hosted coffee talks, and meetings and dinners, all for the purpose of talking about what the problem was at our school. We talked about why it was not appropriate to segregate our students by language. We had presentations about the research that had been done on dual-language programs and how they actually help students who speak primarily English do better in school. We talked about all the support there was for teachers to stretch their skills and earn professional credit for free. We talked about this issue until I was blue in the face.

After a full school year of talking and listening, our participatory management team voted to move forward and implement the dual-language program in the entire school. This was a big deal because the team consisted of members from every part of our school community. Furthermore, this decision affected the entire structure of staff. With this new curriculum delivery model, teachers had to team with each other at every grade level. And classes would now be made up of one-half English-speaking students and one-half Spanish-speaking students. I was excited about the prospect of this program, but the change was big. And I do not think our community would have been behind it had I not spent the entire school year educating everyone about the bigger problem our school had concerning language, race, and class. I also think giving people time to think about the suggested change and to let them share their fears and frustrations concerning change helped. In the end, all those meetings where everybody was involved made a big difference.

Alex's story demonstrates how shuttling back and forth between groups of teachers, parents, and community members is the best way to bring all of the school's stakeholders to the center of an issue. Making clear to each constituency during these discussions what the parameters are concerning their input is most important. The principal's diplomacy, patience, and time are the keys to helping everyone understand and support a change in a school's curriculum. It is also most important to continuously assess where your community is concerning an issue. If you have worked long and hard to win a community over and an issue is still not in favor, consider the importance of respecting the school community's view and wait to see if there is another time to bring the issue forward again. Principal Kelly Ritter's story exemplifies this tactic:

> One school in our district had adopted a student uniform policy with great success. Our district had even passed a governing board policy outlining the procedures to implement a student uniform policy. So I decided to try and see if our school would be willing to adopt this policy. I tried all year; we had meetings and we had fashion shows, I think I put in hundreds of hours of listening to people talk, complain, and question. After ten months of this, we brought the issue to our shared decision-making team. They voted against the idea. So after a year of trying, I dropped it. And then a funny thing happened. A year went by and one of the neighboring schools adopted the policy. A second year went by and another school adopted uniforms for their students. Three years after my community said "no" to a uniform policy, I decided to try again. I utilized the same strategy of meetings and talks and tons of my time one on one with people. This time the community team passed the uniform dress code. Now our students are all in uniform and the policy has indeed made a difference in our school. I am glad we were able to implement this change, but it took more than one try.

Problem Solving

One of the wonderful aspects of a shared decision-making team is that it is a perfect forum for all aspects of a school organization to discover and examine areas of concern or challenge for the school. Sometimes a principal may not even be aware of a particular challenge until he or she has heard multiple perspectives related to the same hard-to-define problem. For example, consider Wendy Sherman's story:

> I had been the principal of this wonderful K-8 school for two years. Our school was located at the end of a small narrow cul-de-sac in the central

business district of a large city. That cul-de-sac was like our own private jewel. The street had about twenty houses on it. There was no street light where it intersected with the main road. As you might guess, the traffic was ridiculous at arrival and dismissal time. Cars were backed up all the way to the main road every morning and every afternoon. We had cross-walks and two crossing guards directing traffic. Sometimes, I would even go out to help manage all the cars.

There was one gate on the back field of the school that allowed children who were walking to school to enter from the back. However, the only student drop-off point and parking lot was located in the front of the campus. Because the traffic got so bad in the cul-de-sac, parents started driving around the block and dropping off their children in the middle of the street that was adjacent to the back gate that allowed for students who walked to school to enter the grounds. The homeowners who lived on the back road began to call and complain that the traffic was disruptive.

We decided that at our next shared leadership team meeting that we would invite everyone in the community to talk about the traffic flow problem. Neighbors, parents, staff members, and a representative from the city planning office came. The neighbors wanted the back gate locked to stop the flow of noisy traffic. The parents refused to lock the gate and wanted to build a new drop-off area. The city planner said it would not be feasible to rezone the street. The neighbors were furious at me for not locking the gate. I maintained that locking the gate was not within my power because this was a decision for the community. In the end, I assigned an aide to stand by the gate before and after school to supervise. We sent notes home to parents encouraging them not to use the back street to drop off their children. Not all of the parents listened and we still have a problem. But at least the community has had a chance to look at this problem from everyone's point of view. Now everyone involved at least understands that it is no one particular person's fault. I don't think all problems in a school are supposed to be solved, but at least as a whole community we are making attempts to examine our challenges from all sides.

Resource Attraction

Community involvement encompasses more than simply including folks in decisions or making sure that concerns are heard by school personnel. A community-centered school also means that the campus itself

serves as the heart of the community. In a very obvious way this is accomplished because a school campus is a central meeting place for organizations such as Boy Scouts and softball leagues. Consider the other
avenues for community involvement by reviewing the questions in figure 7.1.

Increasing Resources and Opportunities for Students   One of
the greatest benefits to community involvement is the increase in resources that are available to your staff to use creatively. These resources
are more than yearly donations from the business owner down the street

---

How Is My School the Heart of the Community?

1. Do we regularly host family math, reading or writing night?

2. Do we celebrate grandparents with an event?

3. Do our students visit or perform at the local nursing home?

4. Do our students partner in some way with our sister high school or
   elementary school (reading to a sister class, etc.)?

5. Do we have an adult and family literacy program?

6. Do we host adult learning classes such as yoga or pottery?

7. Do we host a carnival, cookout, or curriculum fair regularly to
   highlight student success and interaction?

8. Do we utilize our staff for regular presentations for adults one
   evening a month? (For example, a science teacher could give an
   astronomy talk.)

9. Is our library open one evening a week for students and families to
   read together?

Figure 7.1.   Avenues for Community Involvement

from campus. The key to building resources is to first network with all levels of your school community. Encourage your teachers to host one or two parent nights each semester in which they can get to know parents better. Ask for greater help in the form of volunteers in the classroom or with field trips and projects. Help your staff understand that you cannot be the only person who works to bring members of the community on your campus. Parents can be great networking advocates if they understand what is going on in their child's class and if they are excited about it. When your teachers think outside of the box, they can inspire help from their community. Todd Johnson is one such teacher in California. His latest learning adventure for his students involved the construction of a garden:

> I teach seventh grade and our school site is one of those old-fashioned egg crate campuses with breezeways down the center of campus and classrooms that open up to patches of grass in between the buildings. I wanted to try an integrated unit of some sort so I teamed with a fifth-grade teacher, Miss Mason, and we decided to teach both of our classes about Thomas Jefferson by way of constructing a garden on our campus that was like one of the ones at Monticello. My students researched the plants he had and learned what the grounds looked like through the Internet. Miss Mason's students spent time designing how the beds would look. Then we had a meeting one night with both classes and their parents. We explained our project and asked if families would be willing to give a Saturday's worth of work to help build our garden. We passed out a wish list of items and assignments ranging from the construction of tags that identified the genius and species of each plant to digging the trenches for the garden. Three weeks later, all sixty students and their families descended on campus at six in the morning. We worked all day. By the time the sun went down there was this amazing garden on our campus. We held a dedication ceremony the following Monday during school. You know we have had that garden now for four years and no one ever vandalizes it. Every year a different class adds something. And it has grown to be something that includes the whole school. The eighth grade built two benches that were replicas of those Jefferson had made. The first graders designed and made bird feeders. The art class even painted a mural of the view of the grounds of Monticello on a wall near the garden. It has really become a special place on our campus for students, as well as adults, to enjoy.

A campus-improvement project does not have to be the only catalyst for the members of your school community to share its resources. Service-learning projects for students that involve organizations such as Habitat for Humanity are excellent vehicles for students and the community to pool resources and help improve homes or other community sites in your school's neighborhood. Invite service organizations such as Rotary, Kiwanis, veterans' associations, and other civic groups to become more involved with your students and staff as a way to increase the ties between community and school.

How far is the nearest library or museum from your campus? Do not overlook the bounty of resources hungry to partner with schools that are part of your city's cultural scene. Finally, do not overlook small businesses. They are wonderful places to create partnerships that allow students to explore possible career choices and to allow the business some great publicity with their neighborhood. When people talk about the school being the heart of their community, they do not necessarily mean that everything happens at the school site. Schools with strong community ties are usually led by professionals who understand that the school and community need to have a symbiotic relationship.

CHAPTER 7 INSTANT REPLAY: FOCUS ON COMMUNITY INVOLVEMENT

1. Small incidences and miscommunication can snowball quickly into factions of people who feel left out.
2. Creating effective vehicles for community decision depends on true and equal representations of all constituencies in a school community.
3. Have legitimate agendas for your shared decision-making team; do not have a meeting for the sake of saying that you had one.
4. Learn about your district's preferred decision-making model before you try and implement it.
5. Go out of your way to make the community decision-making team's meeting convenient for those involved.
6. Facilitating consensus takes a leader's patience, diplomacy, and time.

7. Brainstorm ideas for community decisions ahead of time with possible answers to explore.
8. Involving the community is more than fund-raising.
9. Realize that sometimes there are problems that are unsolvable in your community.
10. If you are unable to move an agenda item forward with your community, consider the timing of your ideas and do not be afraid to try again at a later date.

8

THE CHANGE
GAME

Debbie Genco sat in the conference room biting her fingernails, waiting for one of her favorite professors, Dr. Jones, to arrive. She had
learned a great deal about leadership and reform in his class, and this
was the first time she would see him since her promotion to an administrative position. She wanted everything to be just perfect for his visit.
"Please let this in-service go smoothly . . . please let this in-service go
smoothly." She mumbled the mantra over and over again until Dr. Jones
walked in.

Debbie popped up from her chair and eagerly shook his hand. "Dr.
Jones, good to see you. I am so pleased you were able to come to our
school to help us align our curriculum to the state standards. Can I get
you a cup of coffee?"

Stephen Jones, a professor with the local university, eagerly shook
Debbie's hand and said, "Oh, not just yet, thank you. But I would love a
place to hang my coat. How long have you been the assistant principal
here? It seems like you were in my class only last year."

"Actually, Dr. Jones, I took your assessment class three years ago. I was
promoted last year to assistant principal. You know, it was our principal
Mrs. Johnson who saw you present at a conference about mapping curriculum to standards in San Francisco last November. She thought you
would be a good facilitator for our faculty. I am glad you remembered
me. Did Mrs. Johnson explain that she had a meeting at the district office?"

"Yes she did, Debbie. My understanding is that today you have scheduled a series of appointments for us with each of your subject-area
teachers by department. And at those appointments, you would like me
to talk to your teachers about the standards and proficiency tests and ask
them to make general maps of what they teach and when. Is that correct?"

"Yes, sir, it is. Each one of our team meetings is an hour long and we
have a thirty-minute break for lunch. I think it is only fair to share with
you that our faculty is a mixture of old guard teachers and professionals
new to the field. To be honest, the conversations we have had about how
state standards impact our curriculum have not been smooth. Some
people really resent the extra work."

Dr. Jones smiled and said, "I know how this is for you, Debbie. Do
not be anxious. You remember from class that people react to change in

different ways. I understand that ultimately, when a visitor comes to campus, it is somewhat like when a guest comes to your home. You want everything to go smoothly. It will. And don't worry about my impressions of your school. It looks to me like you are doing a fine job. Is it time to start?"

Debbie smiled at his comforting analysis of the situation and got up to open the conference room door for the first team meeting. "Dr. Jones, these are the members of our English department: Mrs. Blakely, Mrs. Schuman, Mrs. Cartwright, and Mrs. Dotson."

The teachers shook Dr. Jones's hand and then sat down. Stephen Jones started the diatribe he had been using at all the other high schools he visited:

"Good morning, I am pleased to be here to work with you. I was invited by your principal to facilitate a series of meetings with you and your colleagues, to discuss your curriculum and how to develop a year-long map that demonstrates how your classroom practices are aligned to the state standards. As you know, there has been a requirement from your district that each school submits a schoolwide plan that describes how it is meeting all of the state standards for proficiency tests in the classroom. In front of each of you is a copy of the state standards. At some point during this hour we will be looking at it. But before we do so, I thought what we could do is simply get out a piece of paper and list, off the top of your head, the units that you cover throughout the year in your class. It does not have to be perfectly accurate. Just think for now what you teach in September and then write it down. Then go to October and write what you cover. Continue on for each month . . ."

"Excuse me," interrupted Mrs. Blakely. Debbie curled her toes inside her shoes and thought, "Please don't go there Harriet, just be quiet. I knew you would do this. I knew you would be rude. The man is a guest. Just this once Harriet, can you play nice with others?"

Dr. Jones stopped speaking when Mrs. Blakely interrupted him. He now saw the anger in her face and replied, "I'm sorry, was there something you would like to share?"

"There sure is. I think now is the perfect opportunity to tell you I am not doing a thing for you. I resent the fact that I have to sit here and have someone tell me how to teach who isn't even in a school. I have been teaching for fifteen years and every one of my evaluations is stellar. I resent the government telling me how to do my job. And I have lesson plans to explain what I do."

Dr. Jones replied, "I can certainly understand your frustration with the standards and the district plan, but your principal invited me here to help you with this. And this should only take you a few minutes to jot down what you teach each month. This is only an approximation; it does not have to be detail specific."

The rest of the members of the English department were now looking down at their papers trying to think about what units they taught each month. Mrs. Blakely went on, "I don't think you understood me. I am simply not going to do this. I don't care who asks me. I don't need to."

Debbie was mortified. She did not know what to say. She did not want to get in the middle of the confrontation between Dr. Jones and Mrs. Blakely, and yet she was frustrated that as the new assistant principal she did not have as much clout with the teachers as the principal did. Dr. Jones looked at Mrs. Blakely and said, "If you don't feel a need to participate, that is fine. Your lack of participation is between you and your principal. However, I am responsible for fulfilling her request to facilitate this meeting. So if you don't mind. I'd like to continue."

Mrs. Blakely turned away from Dr. Jones and looked Debbie square in the eye and said, "You know, I was here before these standards and this administration came on board and I'll be here when they leave. The same thing happens every few years. Trot the teachers out . . . make them jump through a bunch of hoops that get in the way of real teaching and then change the rules and expectations. All the mandates for change come and go and you know, as well as I do, that in the end, they have no relevance to what we do every day. It is just a big game. Well this time, you can count me out."

Debbie took a deep breath and thought, "Right now, I hate my job. I am so embarrassed. Why did I ever think that I could bring about reform at this school?"

THE DIRT ON CHANGE

Change is the thing that leaders speak about when addressing the current wrongs of the system they are trying to manage. Numerous volumes have been written about change: How to make it happen, how to deal with it, and why it is or is not a good thing. The crux of the change game that administrative aspirants learn in graduate school is this:

1. School principals work in a pool of political waters that stretch from their neighborhood to the state legislature, to the White House. Any and all parts are affected by the slightest ripple at any point. Thus, the very nature of the principalship requires us to address constant demands or edicts for change, because there is constant ripple in the system somewhere.
2. Principals need to have a game plan congruent with the district vision that everyone buys into before instituting change.
3. Change requires the support of superiors, staff, and community (which is based on fit and relationship building).

In essence, the above truths can best be summed up mathematically (see figure 8.1).

1+2+3= 6 (Effective Change)

Figure 8.1.   The Change Formula

The formula given in figure 8.1 is offered up regularly by aspirants on licensure exams and in job interviews. Unfortunately, the principalship is a job that requires one to learn things by living through them. Thus, only experience teaches a principal that the change formula we learn in college is succinct but not always accurate. A few battle scars teach us to understand that the change formula exists in varying forms (see figure 8.2).

So what is it that alters the results of 1+2+3? Differences in outcome are due to some predictable things, like the motivations for change and the agendas of those leading change. However, unpredictable factors like timing and crisis play a part in the change process. Furthermore, principals begin their terms as leaders in a highly politicized environment with no natural allies. This daunting initiation is the unavoidable

$$1+2+3 = 5 \text{ (A Step Backward)}$$

$$\text{or}$$

$$1+2+3= 1+2+3 \text{ (No Change at All)}$$

Figure 8.2.   The Change Formula in Varying Forms

result of the political chaos caused by the exodus of the principal's predecessor.

The cry for change can occur simply because one wants to move a personal agenda forward. The change saber can also be rattled in order to justify the existence of a leader, a program, or a budget. Worse still, changes can be implemented simply because no one in the organization was able to say to the instigator, "Hey, wait a minute. We should not do this, it is not a good idea and here are the reasons why."

The impetus for change is found in the ripples of the political and systemic waters mentioned earlier. Remember, number one of the change formula states that principals are on the front line of dealing with these waves every day. The key to deciding if the ripples are worth addressing rests in the consideration of the questions in figure 8.3.

One colleague described the principal's struggle to balance change with leadership as a knight on a white horse galloping through a battlefield to rescue the village that is his school. Everyday problems along with edicts for action come in the form of flaming arrows or cannonballs that are shot at him. Sometimes he sees the arrows zooming in head-on, and sometimes they are coming from directions he cannot pinpoint. Through on-the-job training, our noble principal learns to sense when the arrows are coming and how to steer the horse out of their path. However, experience does not guarantee complete protection and sometimes the knight gets injured.

Invest in the prevention and treatment of wounds by being prepared. Part of those efforts should include a solid understanding of the afore-

- Is this change something that I need to facilitate to ensure the safe and orderly environment of my school?

- Do I need the district office to help my staff and community value and support the implementation of this change?

- Will the district office support me in this change?

- Will I be able to hold my staff accountable for implementing this change?

- Do I really have to do something to address this demand for change, or do I need to just demonstrate I am making an effort?

- What are the costs and benefits of implementing this change: to me personally, to my school, and to my district?

Figure 8.3. Questions about Change

mentioned concept of fit in conjunction with time devoted to building relationships with folks who can protect you or feed your network of information. Governing boards and superintendents almost never go after principals who enjoy a strong solid power base in their community and/ or teachers' union.

Principals also look to avoid harm by staying away from decisions that will make waves. One view is that by producing small waves, rather than big ones, improvements can be made within a system over an extended amount of time. This approach is less controversial and can assure a longer term in many systems. The opposite view is that little waves only equal little change. Turning a system completely upside down (or at least in another direction) can be chaotic, but the results can be more dramatic and more obvious.

Both approaches have their advantages and their disadvantages. If you enjoy an occasional tsunami, then you are, in general, someone who boasts a strong political stomach and has no problem moving from one system to another. If you prefer smoother waters, you provide a needed sense of stability and cohesion to a community. Ultimately, the decision of what kind of waves you create rests in your gut. For most leaders, integrity is what helps them choose the types of waves they make or avoid making.

Willard Waller wrote a book in 1938 that linked the change process to the chronology of a person's efforts as a leader. Chapter 5 briefly touches on Walter's belief that a leader's function is to make decisions. However, every decision made by that leader will anger at least one person. Over the course of time, the leader will have made enough decisions to make enough people angry so that he (or she) has worn out his (or her) welcome. No one is happy and no is doing what the leader asks. When that happens, the leader is no longer leading.

This paradox does not always mean all-out mutiny—subordinates often tell their leader one thing and do another because they are afraid of repercussions from their boss. That is why it can be so difficult for principals to gauge how effective they really are as change makers. Essentially Waller is saying that leaders, like milk and bread, have a shelf life and can go stale. The hitch where school leadership is concerned is that principals do not have expiration codes tattooed on the back of their neck.

So how do you know when you are stale? What happens if you have done a great job of galloping away from the arrows and cannonballs only to realize that someone else has cut your horse's legs off?

The first step in answering these questions is to analyze the progression of your term as principal. Chapters of a principal's term at a specific school can be examined like a bell curve. The ascension of the bell's curve is associated with the honeymoon period and the first efforts made by the principal to figure out how to fit. Once fit is achieved, trust and loyalty from different members of the school community follow. It is during this time that the principal begins to reach the peak of his or her ability to institute changes and foster loyalty among staff and community.

The duration of the peak on the curve depends on how the principal deals with the inevitable arrows and cannonballs hailing down around him. At the top of the bell curve is usually where principals decide the kinds and numbers of waves they want to create. This peak of effectiveness on the curve will eventually drop for one of two reasons mentioned previously in chapter 5:

1. Too many people are angry about changes made—therefore they don't support the principal.
2. Too many people are angry because no changes are made—so the principal does nothing—therefore they don't support him.

When 1 or 2 happens, the principal is stale. Multiple factors ranging from making blunders to raising the ire of the teachers' union, to causing one too many headaches for the superintendent can trigger the curve's turn downward. The descending curve reveals the phase in a leader's tenure when he or she no longer fits. From there it is simply a matter of time until someone (or many someones) finds a way to help the principal understand what everyone already knows—it is time to go. Perhaps the most important thing to remember about this curve is that it is not at all related to time. For some leaders this curve represents three years of work, and for others this curve represents thirty.

Despite the day-to-day challenges of school leadership, savvy principals invest in the painful process of reflecting on their tenure, their life goals, and the state of things in their district. Reflecting on a career does not make you a savvy principal: Removing your ego and your sense of idealism while looking hard at your career does. Careful attention should be paid to how you, the leader, are perceived by all the stakeholders in your school and your district. Annually you need to check your gut and ask yourself, "Do I still fit?" If your answer is no, remind yourself that fit is not a measure of excellence as a leader. It is a political term that describes in some ways how effective you are. Keeping this observation in mind, you may want to consider the questions in figure 8.4.

STARTING THE CHANGE BALL ROLLING

Having a command of research and trends in education helps you to build credibility with people you meet, who may not understand the importance of what you are doing. Once you feel comfortable in being able to talk to people about why a quality workforce is dependent on literate adults or the statistics explaining the relationships between literacy and poverty, you need to develop, for your own reference, a mission

- If I don't fit, do I still want to?

- What will it take for me to fit again if that is what I want?

- Am I in the position to choose whether to stay or go?

- Can I live with myself if I stay?

- What can I learn about politics from this experience?

- What could I have done differently?

Figure 8.4.   Questions to Consider

statement. A mission statement is not a long-winded diatribe explaining your philosophy. For purposes of this conversation, a mission statement is simply one to three sentences that for *you, personally,* describe what you are doing.

In order to craft a mission statement, imagine yourself in a coffeehouse; up to your table walks a famous millionaire real-estate developer, his supermodel wife, and their ten-year-old daughter. When the daughter asks you what you do for a living, your mission statement should be the answer to her question. Your mission statement needs to be clear enough so that all three members of this family can understand and remain interested in what you are saying. Your mission statement is also the context that should drive all of your professional decisions.

BUILD A NETWORK OF BELIEVERS

Networking is the art of building contacts and exchanging information with all sorts of people. Leaders will tell you that networking is the most important tool anyone has who is trying to build support for something and bring about change. To discover what sort of network you already have, create the categories listed in figure 8.5 on a piece of paper and then list the names of people you know in each one.

You can increase your categories geographically if you wish to include state and national levels. The next step is to analyze your lists. Where are the shortest lists? These are the places to start brainstorming new names of people whom you need to meet, have lunch with, and talk to about the importance of your mission. Along the lines of meeting people, remember that you never know when you will meet someone who could be a helpful addition to your network. Always be prepared for these opportunities by having your business cards readily available (you might even want to print your mission statement on your cards).

The last category listed earlier is unique to the others in that it is an arena for you to find support and mentorship in fulfilling your mission. People in this category are those who you would want to call to have a mentoring conversation with or to get help from in brainstorming some solutions to challenges you are facing. Obvious organizational choices

- People at various schools that understand and support my mission

- People at the Governing Board Office that understand and support my mission

- Local business owners that understand and support my mission

- Local Agency heads (hospitals, social services, United Way, etc.) that understand and support my mission

- Local fraternal organization heads (Lions Club, Rotary) that understand and support my mission

- Media professionals (television, radio, newspaper) that understand and support my mission

- University personnel that understand and support my mission

- People in professional organizations that can help me

Figure 8.5.   Networking

- Create a yearlong calendar in which your coalition meets once a month (or once every other month). When you make this calendar, think of a goal that you would like to reach by the end of the year. This goal could be that all members of the coalition are more committed to adult literacy, or it could be that by the end of the year you have a program up and going.

- Invite a group of people to be on your coalition that is comprised of 1/3 supporters, 1/3 ambiguous contacts in various categories, and 1/3 naysayers.

- Make sure the ambiguous contacts represent folks who have resources that you need (i.e., money, people, volunteer time, space available for use, etc).

- Make sure at every meeting people are fed and comfortable. (This ensures a better mind-set and more collaboration.)

Figure 8.6.   Reinforcing the Change Process

for this category include the Association for Supervision and Curriculum Development, the International Reading Association, or the National Association for Partners in Education. These are just three of many organizations that have easy-to-find websites, are committed to building partnerships between school and community, and value literacy education.

At the same time you are developing your network lists, you need to create lists of people who are not simply ignorant of your mission but who are opposed to it. These lists will help you identify roadblocks to developing the resources you need to accomplish your mission.

A specific plan that will help reinforce the change process at your school is shown in figure 8.6.

THE FIRST SESSION—MAKING A STRATEGIC PLAN

Once you have a list of people who would make a strong coalition in terms of resources and support, invite them to a meeting to discuss literacy. In order to assure that those invited actually attend, put forth the effort to call and personally deliver invitations.

Begin the first meeting of your decision-making team by having everyone relax with coffee, treats, and small talk. The treats are just as important as the small talk because people tend to be more collaborative when they are fed while working in a comfortable environment. Invite everyone to introduce himself or herself to the group and offer a sentence or two about what brought each one to this meeting. You then explain that the reason for this meeting is to talk about family and adult literacy as it pertains to your community.

Break team members into teams of three or four people each. Make sure that the teams are balanced to include a representative from each sector in your community. For example, have one educator, one business leader, and one social services head on a team. Give each team a large piece of chart paper and have them list all the reasons why the change proposed at your school is an inconvenient or unnecessary investment. Each group picks their top two answers and gives them to you. Bring your small groups back together as a large group and ask for the top two answers.

Write these answers on another piece of large chart paper so that the group ends up with a list that represents the thinking of the entire coalition. After completing this exercise, regroup the participants back into small groups. Have the groups brainstorm all the challenges that happen at your school as a result of the problems that are demanding the change you want to make. Again, have each small group pick the top two, bring the groups back together, and make a list representing the entire coalition.

The next step is to facilitate a discussion with the entire group that helps the coalition members realize the long-term benefits of the change you are interested in implementing. This discussion will probably take some time and energy. (It may even require multiple meetings just to focus on education about the necessity of the change and how it will affect stakeholders.)

When appropriate, give the group a break to recharge. The length of the break provided should be sensitive to the needs of the participants and can range from an hour lunch to twenty minutes depending on the amount of time and resources available.

When the break is over, reassign the participants to new groups. Changing group structure is important because it alters group dynamics and attitudes, as well as takes the emotionality out of the discussion.

After affirming the good work done before the break, check to see if all (or a majority) of the participants have bought into the belief of the global concept that your change can bring. The final step is to have the newly formed small groups brainstorm ways to realistically implement and build support for the proposed change. (Here, again, this may take more than one meeting.) Each small group picks the top two, then as a large group, look at the list created. This final list is essentially the coalition's short- and long-term strategic plan. It should also serve as a template for determining the year's meetings and agendas.

Following up a strategic planning session with thank-you notes is wise, along with a note to the newspaper reporter who covers education and local community issues. The strategic planning session that is described here can be stretched over two or even ten meetings. The time it takes to complete a strategic plan is directly related to the group of people whom you are with. It is extremely important to begin to schedule one-on-one time with each of these members to simply chat and build a relationship. Use these moments not to give a hard sell but to really try to get to know the person. Demonstrating an interest in another person's world helps to build credibility on your part as well as extends the depth of your working relationship. One of the most important aspects to becoming a successful lobbyist for support of any program is to remember that garnering support is analogous to a marathon—not a fifty-yard dash. Consistency and credibility are the keys, particularly in the areas of building and maintaining relationships within your network and convincing naysayers to change their minds.

ASSESSMENT

The final component to any quality plan for change is one that centers on the assessment of its efficacy. Essentially the assessment components can be broken down into small and large factors that mark your school's progress down the change path. The change process is analogous in many ways to a road trip. The first thing you do concerning a road trip is to decide where you want to go. Then, you gather the supplies you need to get you and your car there efficiently and comfortably. Next, you find a map and use it to look for road signs and other topographical markers that demonstrate you are on your way. Finally, you know when you have reached your destination because there are other more prominent signs.

Follow this same metaphor when you construct your change plan with your decision-making team. Brainstorm with your team what the signs will be that your school is on the right path with your change. Markers that demonstrate to stakeholders your vigilance to the change path can range from an increase in student standardized test scores for a particular curriculum change to a decrease in discipline issues with a new addition to the student handbook.

Make sure that the stakeholders are reminded regularly what the road markers are for change, so that as your school embarks down the road to change, you can celebrate whenever you find these markers in the school. Because the change process can be slow or controversial, it is important to celebrate reminders of its success with the community. This builds more support for the change-making decisions you instituted in the first place.

CHAPTER 8 INSTANT REPLAY: THE CHANGE GAME

1. The principalship requires constant attention to demands for change.
2. Change requires the support of superiors, subordinates, staff, and community.
3. Make sure your change plan is congruent with your district's values.
4. Take the time to assess if a change is truly needed and worth making.
5. Invest in reflecting on your own shelf life and your ability to make change.
6. Articulate a change plan that is easily repeated and understood by the community.

7. Network, network, network.
8. Allow your decision-making team the time they need to understand why your proposed change is important and relevant.
9. Follow up on your strategic planning meetings with individual relationship-building efforts.
10. Build assessments as to your school's progress down the change path so that all stakeholders can see the relevance and value of the changes being made.

9

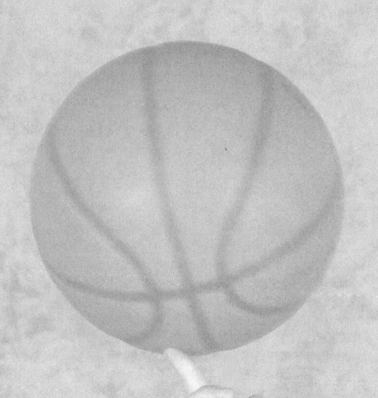

FINDING
BALANCE

Carl Hurlburt, a career school administrator and decorated Vietnam veteran, was pacing around the deck of his swimming pool. He had his hands clasped behind his back and was trying to think through the latest problems with his school district's contract negotiations process. He muttered something about the union being a pain, walked a little faster, and then squinted his eyes.

His wife, Jeanne, a school principal, brought his attention away from reliving the arguments and memos of contract negotiations by asking, "Carl . . . Would you please get over here and turn the steaks? I don't want them to burn. Gwen is inside getting the wine glasses for us. Are you still wondering about work?" Carl chose to focus only on his wife's request and answered, "Yes, baby girl, I'm coming over. Where are the tongs?"

Gwen arrived on the patio just in time to answer, "They are on the grill plate. If they had been a snake—they would have bit you." Carl fumbled for the tongs and said,

"Now I ask you ladies, is this a beautiful evening, or what? We've got the good music on the stereo, the orange trees are blossoming, and the stars are starting to come out. How much better can it get?"

Jeanne smiled a Cheshire cat smile and said, "Sweetie, you do understand that you are not fooling your wife or your dinner guest with your observance of this nice spring night. We both know that you are still fixated on work."

Carl chided back, "Well, now, the pacing helps me to think and it is a pretty night out. And, Gwen, you know I am thrilled to see you. What's it been, about six hours since we sat together at leadership council?"

This time it was Gwen's turn, "Hey, you guys invited me. And you know work is work and play is play. Besides, I am not the one thinking about the trash from today's meeting. My administrator hat is off."

Carl responded to Gwen's quip with a hug and said, "You know, you are one of our favorite people. If you'll forgive me and find the bottle opener for the wine, I promise to be good."

Gwen laughed and said, "OK, you are forgiven. I just would like to see you have a little balance in your life. You know, I have these great relaxation tapes. You could listen to them and they would help you detox from the day."

Carl answered back, "I'm balanced. Aren't we having a lovely dinner? Can't you smell the orange blossoms? It's only every now and then I think about the people who live to make my job difficult at the expense of our students."

"Carl, you know balance is more than dinner with friends. Even now, you are still fixated on what you need to do as the assistant superintendent. A relaxation tape would do wonders for you. Or maybe you could try a little yoga. The positions work your muscles out and you leave feeling lighter and more empowered. I think I read in yesterday's paper there is a new studio opening by your house."

Carl grinned, "Look out. . . . Here comes our resident shaman with her insights to enlightenment. Preach on Mother Earth, just remember I don't do this 'woo-woo' crap."

Both women started laughing at his typically acerbic and humorous response to all things esoteric. In many ways, Carl was still a concrete-thinking soldier who delighted in strategy and politics. He worked hard, he played hard, and he was not afraid to speak his mind. He was known among his friends as a gracious host, a loyal friend, and extremely ethical. The dinner party on Carl and Jeanne's patio ended with the usual jokes about Gwen's commitment to yoga and his halfhearted promise to think about "woo-woo" crap in the greater context of his life as a school administrator.

Three weeks after Gwen sent a "thanks for dinner" note to Carl and Jeanne, she was in the parking lot of Baptist Memorial Hospital, pulling a teddy bear out of the backseat of her car along with a stack of magazines. She walked quickly down the halls with her arms full of these gifts, looking for the signs that read "Coronary Care Unit." When she finally reached the unit, the curtain around bed number two slid open to reveal a drowsy assistant superintendent full of morphine.

"Hi sweetie," Carl slurred.

Gwen put the teddy bear on the tray by Carl's bed and said, "And hello to you. I brought you a new little friend to keep you company. And here are some magazines for Jeanne." She could not help but think about how vulnerable her boss looked. That small white gown and chest tubes robbed Carl of his aura as the resident tough guy.

A technician interrupted with, "Excuse me, Mr. Hurlburt? It's time to roll you over. We need to take an EKG before surgery. Are you ready?"

"Yes sir. Ready sir. Yes sir."

Gwen could only smile at how Carl gave his answer. Even now, in this state of half consciousness, her friend was still a soldier and still tough. As the EKG machine was ticking away, Jeanne came into the room. "Gwen, what are you doing here? How did you get out of work?"

Gwen hugged her friend, " Do you really think that I would get a message that Carl had a heart attack and I wouldn't drop everything? You two are my dearest friends. Are you OK? I brought you some magazines. Is there anything I can do? Is there anything he needs?"

Jeanne held her husband's hand and said, "Oh . . . A little balance might be nice." Carl half opened his eyes and growled, "I think it's time for 'woo-woo' crap."

Unfortunately, Carl's story is a familiar one to the many administrators who sincerely look to find balance only after a life-threatening wake-up call. After his stay in the hospital, Carl made several changes in his life. They were difficult in some ways because they meant changing the way he thought about himself in terms of his physical capabilities, his job, and how he dealt with stress. He fully recovered from his coronary surgery and now enjoys the benefits of a much healthier life. His friends even now tease him because he is a fully converted believer in the importance of guide imagery and uses relaxation tapes to help himself focus and unwind.

The difficulty in finding balance for many administrators lies in the fact that most of us are by nature people who enjoy the fast-paced challenges that a career in leadership provides. Couple this working environment with a leader's inherent drive to "do it all" and the result is usually a toxic mix of external and self-imposed stressors. Most administrators choose to face these stressors by missing sleep, ignoring proper nutrition, and failing to get enough exercise. Why does this happen when almost everyone in school leadership can recite the tenets of a healthy life? (You know this mantra, it goes like this, "I will eat healthier, I will sleep more, I will exercise. . . .")

Of course reciting what needs to happen to be healthy and actually engaging in healthy behavior are two different things. Leaders ignore the common sense approach to a healthy life because of the "get this done right now" pressures found in the daily schedule of the principalship. The purpose of this chapter is to help you understand that you must take some time to think about finding balance in your career as a principal or you will burn out.

The first step to considering the concept of balance and how it is related to your life is to consider your life into the following large categories in figure 9.1 below.

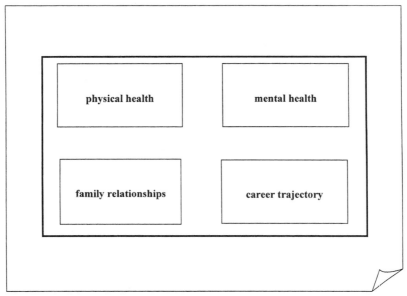

Figure 9.1. Four Aspects of Your Life

The rest of this chapter is devoted to exploring each category.

PHYSICAL HEALTH

For many people when the focus of a conversation turns to physical health the first thing people think about is their weight. One of the most overwhelming problems in our nation is weight management. The problem for administrators is that because the daily schedule is basically a series of meetings interrupted by a series of chaotic crises, finding time to eat properly is difficult. Anita, a principal in her fifth year offers this story:

> I was a PE teacher before I became an administrator. And before that I was a college athlete. When I was in the gym teaching kids, or coaching on the field, I never sat down. In a lot of ways, my job then was great for my health because I was so active. Sometimes I would bring my lunch and sometimes I went out for fast food; either way, I burned everything off by the end of the day. So basically, I did not have to work out. My job was my

workout. When I became an assistant principal, I found the same kind of dynamic: I ran around the school all day chasing kids and never got a chance to sit down. Sometimes I brought lunch, and sometimes I did not. I never got a chance to eat my lunch anyway because there is no time to be still. My first year as a principal, I put on twenty pounds and didn't even realize it. It was like I just turned around one day and my clothes were getting tight.

After I thought about it, I realized that as a principal I sit more. I am in meetings more. And at almost every meeting there is food. Bagels, cookies, punch, you name it. I was too busy to pack a lunch and could not get out of the building to get something to eat so I was eating whatever was around because I was hungry. The worst was when I started to learn that everybody has something they made that they want to bring the principal. Sometimes it is cookies in Mrs. Corwin's class or it is banana nut bread that the secretaries brought or macaroni casserole for teachers' conferences. Part of the culture of a school is that when folks bring food in they save a little for the principal to be nice.

I also realized the problem was that I was not as physically active as I used to be and I was eating everything on the run. So I decided to make some changes. And it was a pain because it required me to plan. I put a small refrigerator in my office and stocked it with water bottles. Every morning I packed a healthy lunch and I started looking for ways to eat that lunch in peace and quiet for fifteen minutes. I would close my door and tell my secretary I need to work on something for fifteen minutes and that I did not want to be disturbed. Sometimes my fifteen minutes was at ten in the morning and sometimes it was at two in the afternoon. But I made sure that every day I had a little time to eat right.

I kept attending the teachers' luncheons. I just would not eat things that I felt were not healthy. I did not want to offend anyone. To be honest there were times when I would fill a plate of whatever casserole someone had made—but I would not eat it. When people brought me treats I would say thank you and wait until the right moment to throw it away. I thought it would be kind of rude to just refuse a food gift. But I decided I did not have to eat a cookie just because someone gave it to me. And I think the water helped. I always seemed to have a bottle of water in my hand. I could carry that to a meeting and sip on it whenever everyone else was going for the treats that were out.

I lost about ten pounds watching my food in about three months, but I could not get off any more. That is when I decided that I had to exercise too. I tried running at first, which I sort of liked. But it was hard to get up at four in the morning to run. Running outside, alone, at eleven at night did not appeal to me either. I hated going to the gym because I would in-evitably see someone I knew. Eventually I bought a treadmill. What a great investment! I can run whenever I want, in the safety of my house and not worry about it. In four more months, I was back to my teaching weight and I felt better. It only took two weeks to shake my craving for fast food; once I gave it up, I didn't even miss it. The hardest part in all of this was finding the time to pack a meal or snacks and water for my fridge. Now I think I am healthier than I have ever been.

The most important lesson from Anita's story is that she made the investment in planning. She planned the food she was going to eat, the time to eat it, and how she was going to deal with situations where food was present in which she did not want to yield to its temptation. Anita also tried several strategies to include a program of physical ex-ercise in her day. While a treadmill may not be the answer for you, there are other strategies to consider in order to add some physical ac-tivity to your day. Another beloved veteran principal of a K-8 school solved her problem of meshing exercise with work by coming to work at six in the morning. She then would complete tasks at her desk, meet with teachers, and generally get the school day off and rolling until 9 AM. On the days in which there were no 9 AM meetings, this principal would leave her office and exercise at the club down the street from her school. She would do a round of circuit training and get back to her school by 10:30 AM. While this approach is not for everyone, par-ticularly those principals who need to prove themselves to the com-munity, it did work for her.

Many principals combine a little mental rest and relaxation with physical activity by walking the perimeter of their campus with em-ployees at lunch. By setting up a walking club, you are able to add a new dimension to your relationships with your employees and get some physical activity at the same time. You might consider regularly exer-cising with the students at your school. A high school principal in Cleveland plays basketball on Tuesdays and Thursdays at lunchtime with any students who are interested. By allowing for exercise time within your day and including others such as students or staff, you also hold yourself to a higher level of accountability. You are more likely to exercise if you know other people are sharing the experience with you. Ultimately, what is important is that you engage in physical activity with consistency and at a level that is appropriate to you.

MENTAL HEALTH

Because our culture still places several taboos on the subject of mental health, people tend to wince when they consider this topic. The paradigm for many seems to be either you are a crazy person or you are not. Counselors, and other trained mental health professionals, are slowly beginning to help Americans realize that mental health covers a spectrum of issues that directly relate and affect leadership performance. These areas range from stress to depression, to anxiety.

When considering your own mental health, remember that your priorities must lie in keeping yourself healthy in order to facilitate a healthy working environment for others. Begin with the simplest of considerations by using the questions in figure 9.2 to think about how your workspace is organized.

Another helpful insight into maintaining a healthy attitude and lowering your work-related stress is to observe the practice of setting boundaries. One of the most trite and dangerous phrases in the administrative lexicon is "My door is always open." If you choose to say this and observe this practice, the result will be that you will never have time for yourself. If you use this phrase and are not regularly available to people who want to see you immediately, you will be seen as a principal who is not credible.

Find a middle ground by letting your secretaries know that when your office door is open, you are willing to meet with anyone who would like to talk to you. When it is closed, you would prefer that staff wishing to speak to you talk with your secretary to make an appointment or leave a message. Meetings do not have to be the only reason to close your door. Sometimes, ten minutes of undisturbed quiet time in your office can rejuvenate your perspective. Helping your staff to understand that you are more than willing to meet with them *on your terms* helps to set parameters of respect.

Another lesson concerning boundaries is usually learned after time in the principal's chair. New principals often feel as though projects or events will not go as planned unless they are present. You do not have to attend everything that happens on your campus. Delegate some of these public relations responsibilities to your assistants. The school really will run without you.

How Healthy Is My Workspace?

1. Do I regularly (once a week) make an effort to tidy up the papers on my
   desk and clean my office?

2. Have I put any energy into making my office my own, through a thoughtful
   display of personal objects or art?

3. Do I need to have my office repainted or repaired in any way?

4. Do I keep a healthy distraction to play with when someone is yelling at me on
   the phone, such as a photo album of happy memories, a desk widget to fiddle
   with, or a favorite magazine?

5. Do I have a CD player and CDs or a sound machine that makes white noise
   or ocean sounds?

6. When is the last time I have purged my office of outdated books, manuals
   and other things that take up space?

7. Can I take advantage of a lamp rather than fluorescent lighting?

8. Is my desk chair comfortable?

9. Is my refrigerator stocked with healthy snacks for me?

10. Have I got a candle or aromatherapy infuser in my office to combat some of
    the more unpleasant school smells that lurk in my building?

Figure 9.2. Questions about Your Workspace

When considering your home phone number and your cell phone, know that if you give them out regularly to people, you can assure yourself the phone will ring. Remember that you do not have to answer the phone just because it rings. Callers' views of appropriate calling times and days can be as diverse as any other opinions that people have. This can also be said of your superintendent. Superintendents, like many other school administrators, can decide to call you about a problem and then engage you in a lengthy conversation that is really not business related. People who do not have a sense of balance in their life blur the lines of work and home. They, too, can forget that just because they want to talk about a problem and share district gossip—you may not. Be careful in these waters as you do not want to offend your superior. However, if you do see a pattern in which you feel that your personal time is interrupted, make a point to listen to the message your caller leaves, and then find ways to strategize your return phone call to honor your own personal time.

STRESSFUL EVENTS AND YOU

Sometimes you may encounter events or times in your career in which you are required to endure extreme stress in your personal and/or professional life while continuing to perform for your building. Examples of this would be a death in the family or a divorce. When you are faced with stressful events, remember that by talking about them with a subordinate, you are guaranteeing the public knowledge of your problems in your school. Look for friends and colleagues outside of your work world to lean on to ensure that your personal life is not fodder for the gossip mill. Another option that many eschew is counseling. Counseling does not mean that you are crazy or that you will have to be involved with a therapist for years. Often it can be a short-lived experience that helps you to refine your perspective and recharge your soul.

There are even counseling professionals who specialize in working with corporate leaders with issues related to leadership. If you think you would benefit from such an experience, call the counseling department at your university and ask a member of the faculty who they would recommend for your needs. The nice thing about this strategy is that you can even remain anonymous. Everyone at some point in their life has to deal with traumatic events or baggage. A counselor can give you the support you may not even realize you need. Kala, a career school administrator, shares her view on counseling:

> I am one of those people who always did *good*. I was a good girl, a good student, a good wife, and a good teacher. I enjoyed being popular with my colleagues. And then I became a principal. Suddenly I met folks who did not like me. I could not understand what happened. I had not changed; I was still me. But I started to decide that there must be something wrong with me

because not everyone liked me. I started to feel horrible about myself and my job was no fun. I hated work because no matter how hard I tried, I felt like I was not effective because I was not popular with my staff. And then, my marriage unraveled because basically we did not spend any time together. I felt like a total failure. A friend of mine recommended a therapist.

When I called him on the phone I told him not to expect me to role-play with the chair or talk to puppets. I had all these horrible visions of what counseling was like. He took me on as a client despite my warnings. I started going to see him once a week for an hour. The first thing I learned from him was to change my perspective and to not assume that just because some of my staff members were angry that it was my fault. He helped me to see the greater context of the politics of my school and of my district. It took a while, but the work I did in counseling started to sink in. My marriage was not saved, but then it should not have been.

I ended up crawling out this hole where I felt like a failure and learning some wonderful lessons about myself and my role in my school. I stopped therapy after a year and I think it was the best gift I ever gave myself. I know lots of folks who think that going into therapy is a sign of weakness. I think they don't have a clue as to what they are talking about. My work with a counselor helped me to shift my entire life. I am now happily remarried and work in a much happier and sane environment. Going into counseling is not something I routinely share with people; it is still a private thing for me. But I am so glad I took that first step.

TOXIC ENVIRONMENTS AND PEOPLE

One of the things that will often put an administrator (or anyone for that matter) in a state of mental stress is the unwitting participation in a toxic environment. Part of setting boundaries is learning how to recognize a toxic environment. To do that, consider the questions in figure 9.3.

When you make and follow a pledge to yourself that you will rid your life of toxic people, you will generally take yourself out of a toxic environment. Of course, there are times when you will have to deal with these people. But the less you do the better. A toxic person is not just the one alluded to in the questionnaire in figure 9.3. Toxic people can also be the folks who simply never have anything good to say. They may look for ways to perpetuate their own anxiety or misery at your expense. While you are indeed seen as the matriarch or patriarch of your school, you do not have to be the therapist for others. Do not allow yourself to

---

Recognizing a Toxic Environment

- Am I routinely part of a circle of people that spends a considerable amount of time complaining and gossiping?

- Am I routinely part of a circle of people that self-medicates with alcohol, drugs, or food, to deal with the stress in their lives?

- Do I work in an environment in which my colleagues function with integrity?

- Do I work in an environment in which my superiors authentically support me to effectively carry out my job responsibilities?

- Is there a part of my life in which all I do is fight with someone, be it a colleague, spouse, or partner?

- If I needed to disconnect from work for one day, would I be able to without repercussions?

- Do I exist in an environment in which I am routinely degraded, used, or humiliated?

Figure 9.3.   Recognizing a Toxic Environment

get sucked into this situation. Perhaps the hardest part of learning to rid your life of toxic people is to realize that in some instances, you cannot help someone and you need to let their issues go. This may cost you some friendships. If that is the case ask yourself why you would want to maintain a friendship with a person who is toxic to you in the first place.

The flip side of the above warning is built on the advice to look for people and environments that leave you energized. If "energized" seems a little too much like a "self-help therapy" sort of word for you, think of it in these terms: Find environments and people that you want to be a part of that leave you feeling good about what you do and who you are doing it with.

If your work environment is toxic and you are not ready to find another job, find a hobby to balance your life. Find a hobby to balance your life anyway. Learning something new is always a great way to maintain balance in your life and leave you excited about your world. Join the local hiking or photography club. Pick up a new language like Italian, or learn to paint. Anything new to your senses that is entertaining will expose you to new groups of people and feed your soul. And, of course, these types of efforts reduce stress and support mental health.

YOUR MORAL COMPASS, FIT, AND TOXICITY

Another area for reflection when seeking balance in the principalship is the relationship your moral compass has with the environment in which you work. A moral compass is the instrument that serves us throughout our lives when making decisions. Its reference points are used in our professional as well as personal triumphs, crises, and failures. One could further contend that the functioning parts of a moral compass are the bits of wisdom that one garners throughout a lifetime. These bits of wisdom can be more clearly described as a multidimensional set of reference points resulting from a person's experiences and environment. This set of references is what Teresa de Laurentis (as cited in Aegerter, 2000) describes as a Matrix of Identity. The Matrix of Identity consists of a series of "subject positions" that are determined by the context in which we exist. Picture the Matrix of Identity as something like the forms parents fill out when registering their child for the new school year (figure 9.4).

Aegerter describes these "contexts" as the blanks we fill in with answers based on our life experiences. The contexts can change as our life experiences change. That is why, for example, a person might claim one particular political party of philosophy at one point in his or her life and then claim another party at a different time in his or her life.

This author proposes that the amalgamation of the moral compasses of the members of a school system form the basis of its culture. Therefore, you need to pay particular attention to how your moral compass is calibrated in relation to those around you in your school and in your district. If your compass is not in alignment, you will not fit. Do not mistake a lack of fit with meaning that your compass is not calibrated

MATRIX OF IDENTITY (Aegerter, 2000)

Subject Positions	Context
Race	
Gender	
Culture	
Nationality	
Ethnicity	
Geographical or Regional Identity	
Rural or Urban Background	
Sexuality	
Spirituality	
Physical Health	
Mental Health	
Age	
Education	
Profession	
Marital Status	
Parental Status	
Familial Positioning	
Religion	
Language	

Figure 9.4.   The Matrix of Identity (Aegerter, 2000)

properly. It simply means that those around you have a different value set and perspective than you do. The difference between you and your environment may be so small that there will be little to no impact on your relationship with others. However, the inequity may exist to such a degree that you will eventually feel one of two ways about your work environment. The first perspective is that you work in a corrupt environment and you are weary of being asked (or forced) to participate in events that you find unethical. The second perspective is that you work in an environment where people are constantly judging and scrutinizing your choices as a leader. Either scenario is toxic and can lead to burnout. In either situation you need to seriously consider a plan of action to move to another system or school. Recognizing that you no longer fit, that your environment is toxic, and deciding to move on is not a failure. It is actually quite common for many principals and superintendents to move from system to system. Oftentimes a shift in career or environment gives you the chance to start again. Many administrators have experienced a mediocre run in one system only to enjoy stellar success once they relocated to a different one.

These professionals discovered that the benefits of starting over outweigh the inconvenience of change.

FAMILY RELATIONSHIPS

The first aspect of a new principal's balanced life that usually suffers is the time spent with his or her spouse, and/or children. Like all newly appointed executives, principals want to give more than 100 percent of themselves to their new position or school community in order to start their administration off on the right foot. This extra effort translates into extra night meetings and weekend events because new principals instinctively want to connect with as many people as possible. Furthermore, dedicated administrators are in danger of falling into the common trap of bringing their work home, be it in the form of paperwork done at the kitchen table or in the form of per-severating about work issues instead of giving attention to loved ones.

All of the earlier described pitfalls add up to one thing: less time to keep family relationships healthy, functional, and strong. Be cognizant of how easily your work responsibilities can creep into your personal life. By making your personal life top priority, you are guaranteeing that you are healthier and happier at work. Thus, you can give more to your community. Setting boundaries to guarantee healthy family time is not selfish—it is an investment in your sanity. If you fail to draw these sorts of boundaries between your work world and your personal world, you risk alienating those closest to you who provide you with the greatest sense of stability. In order to keep this from happening, reflect on the insights given in figure 9.5.

CAREER TRAJECTORY

Perhaps the greatest gift that successful school administrators have is perspective. They understand that the principalship is a marathon sport rather than a fifty-yard dash. They also realize that the principalship is prone to the unique jobs in which you have to learn by making mistakes. Therefore, do not let your mistakes clutter your focus or your mind. After you reflect on what you have learned from your mistakes, let them

Maintaining Balance with Your Family

Make a point to talk to your family members about how your new job may affect the time you spend with them.

Set aside one night a week just for you and your spouse to have time together, alone.

Set aside one night or morning per week just to spend time with your children.

Embrace the idea that it is a good thing to occasionally bow out of a meeting or event commitment in order to be with your family.

Do not treat your spouse as your therapist.

Do not take more than 30 minutes to talk about work when you get home.

Do paperwork at home on a specified day at a specified time, rather than every night.

Ask family members to bring it to your attention when you backslide into perseverating at home about work.

Figure 9.5.   Insights on Maintaining Balance with Your Family

go. Great coaches usually have ten or twenty fables saved up for their teams about perseverance. These stories are sometimes about how Michael Jordan was not selected as member of his ninth-grade basketball team and yet became the greatest basketball player in the history of the sport. Or they might be historically referenced such as the parable of Abraham Lincoln and all the elections he lost before becoming one of this country's most beloved presidents. A final tale of lifetime achievement is about Albert Einstein, one of the greatest mathematical minds of the twentieth century, who failed geometry in high school. The common theme in all of these stories is that the person who is featured in the story is tenacious: He (or she) does not give up. The person continues to follow what he or she believes is his or her own mission in life.

Chester Barnard described in his seminal book on leadership *The Functions of the Executive* (1940) this quality of perseverance as one of the commonalities that great leaders share.

In order for you to build an internal sense of tenacity in terms of your own career as a leader, you need to first determine what your career trajectory is. In simpler terms, ask yourself what you want to be when you grow up. Is the principalship the pinnacle of your career in education or a stepping-stone to a superintendent's role or other district-level position? Perhaps you see yourself becoming a professor and training other aspiring administrators. Or maybe you would like to start your own consulting firm and work with school districts. Perhaps a career as a lobbyist for various educational causes appeals to you. Some people enjoy being career principals and find change by serving new school communities every few years. Whatever your goals are, make sure you reconnect with them regularly and check to see if your career is unfolding in a way that helps to get to that ultimate goal.

A sound method that encourages you to find perspective on your career is to keep a journal of your reflections. You can fill this out at the beginning or end of every semester. For reflective questions to ponder, see figure 9.6.

Realizing that your career path is one that requires regular foresight is a gift that will serve you well throughout your principalship. Learn to recognize the networking opportunities that come your way. Take advantage of them and consider these moments investments in your future. Do not be afraid to move. Often principals have the mind-set that they aspire to be a leader in a particular community. Open yourself to a wider range of opportunities by considering the benefits of moving to another town, county, or state. Moving does not have to always entail geography. Ask yourself if you are willing to be a principal at a grade level other than the one that you already serve. Are you willing to move from an elementary school to a middle school principalship? If your goal is to someday become a superintendent of a unified district, you should be willing to make such a move as it rounds out your resume. Also consider the benefits of taking a promotion in a smaller community and then returning to a large community to apply for a higher level after you have experience. This concept of "farming out" has been in practice for years and is often taken advantage of by principals looking to move up to district-level positions.

Career Trajectory Reflective Journal Questions

1. What did I learn this semester?

2. Do I still like where I work?

3. Do I want to be here next year?

4. Do I have ideas to take this school forward next year?

5. Whom did I meet or network with that can help me eventually move to the next level in my career?

6. Do I need to consider getting a Ph.D. or other credentials in order to stay on my career trajectory?

7. If the answer to number six is 'yes,' when do I think I will be able to go back to graduate school?

8. What mistakes will I avoid in the future?

9. What are some things I did last semester that I should congratulate myself all over again for doing?

10. Have my career goals changed in the last semester? If so, how?

Figure 9.6. Career Trajectory Reflective Journal Questions

CHAPTER 9 INSTANT REPLAY: FINDING BALANCE

1. Balance is more than working hard and playing hard.
2. A little "woo-woo" crap is a good thing.
3. Set boundaries between your work life and your family life.
4. Invest in making your workspace reflective of you and comfortable to be in.
5. Eat right, sleep right, and exercise.
6. Set aside a night a week for a date with your significant other.
7. Set aside regular time each week for you and your children.
8. Involve your family in school functions whenever appropriate.
9. Think of the long term when considering your career.
10. Learn to wrap you head around the fact that you cannot control everything.

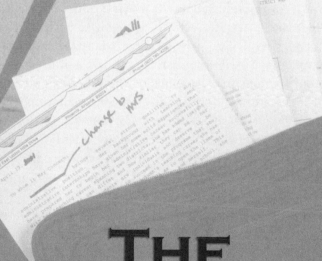

10

THE
LETTER
ARSENAL

The members of Paradise Valley Unified School District's Administrative and Internship Mentoring (AIM) program began their monthly meeting with the usual welcome speech made by Toby Spessard. Mr. Spessard, the district's assistant superintendent, was in charge of this program. The AIM program's purpose was to find and develop a pool of aspiring administrators. A small percentage of the teachers interested in the AIM program were offered membership every June, after a lengthy application process. Those accepted were given two years of training and a chance to intern at schools of their choice. This program was good for the district because it identified new talent and inculcated aspirants to the culture of the district. Teachers wishing to assume leadership positions valued the program because it gave them an opportunity to showcase their talents and get the attention of their superiors.

The agenda for tonight's meeting was a panel discussion about personnel issues with four veteran principals. Three of the four principals serving on the panel were graduates of the AIM program. All four administrators had earned reputations as effective and charismatic leaders.

Mr. Spessard concluded his opening remarks and shifted to the introduction of the panel. "We are lucky this evening to have with us four of Paradise Valley's finest principals. I thought I would begin our introductions by spending some time sharing with you a little bit about what significant contributions they have made as principals in our district."

While Mr. Spessard went on to talk about the achievements of each member, Haley Lynn, an aspirant and new member of the AIM program, could not hear him. She had focused her attention to the events of the day. It was getting more difficult for her to balance her family, her work, and her efforts in graduate school. Frankly, her feet hurt and she was tired.

Haley knew these meetings were important. She also had a sense that this program was more than a training ground. It seemed to her that even though this was called a training program, this was also a competitive arena. She watched her fellow aspirants find new and interesting ways to show their strengths to Mr. Spessard as well as any other district administrator who crossed their path. She also watched her colleagues blatantly suck up. Occasionally she found the whole thing a little too much. Tonight was one of those nights. She felt that the unspoken stress of this evening's meeting was that this was not like the classes she was taking at the university, where she could relax as a student. In her view, the politics of this event mandated thoughtful questions and attention to every detail of the course, even down to what she wore. On AIM meeting days, Haley made a point to wear the same uniform she saw modeled by her administrators: an expensive business suit and dress heels. No one had told her to spend her small teacher's salary on these clothes, but Haley believed that if you wanted to be seen as a serious contender for an administrative position you needed to look like a leader.

Haley had begun to plan her summer job search and needed to ask Mr. Spessard for a letter of recommendation, but she had yet to find the nerve to broach the subject. She kept listening to the panelists talk about their challenges while wondering about her request.

After forty minutes, the time had come for questions from the audience. Haley scrambled to think of something cogent. Unfortunately, she was still fixated on her personal issue of the letter of recommendation. Finally, she had a moment of clarity and raised her hand. When she was called on, Haley politely asked, "I was wondering if each of the panel members could explain a little bit about how they balance all the requests they get for letters of recommendation from staff. I realize that not everyone who asks for a letter is a stellar employee. So how do you deal with that? Do you just turn some people down? If someone is great, how much do you say without sounding insincere? And finally, could someone explain to me how you write a letter for someone who is just average?"

The answers to Haley's questions encompass several letter-writing strategies that apply to areas more global than letters of reference. This chapter is written for those folks who do not consider themselves writers by nature. If you are such an administrator, you will know it because you dread any task that involves the responsibility of writing. In case you are still wondering about your stance on writing, reflect on your experiences in graduate school. Did you enjoy completing writing assignments? When you got your syllabus for a new class, did you go immediately through it and groan when you saw that a twenty-page paper was required? When you do try and start a writing project, do you find yourself staring at a blank computer screen or tablet? If you answered yes to any of these questions, then this chapter is for you. If you are a hardworking principal who finds it difficult to write a smooth letter to the community in the midst of the stresses of the day, then you too will enjoy this chapter. The purpose of this section is to provide you with example letters to inspire you or for you to blatantly plagiarize for your own use.

THE LETTER OF REFERENCE

Letters of reference are taxing because they require your time. Some administrators choose to write glowing letters for anyone who asks. The problem comes when someone who is clearly mediocre, or even worse, incompetent, asks for a letter. Then what do you write? The best way to handle the letter of reference situation is to have three templates on your computer, an A letter, a B letter, and a C letter. Use the A letter template for those employees who are stellar, the B letter template for your average employees, and the C letter template for everyone else. Also know that you can simply refuse to write a letter of recommendation when someone asks. There may be repercussions for you in terms of gossip through the staff, because school culture is often based on the idea that letters of recommendation are a given. Figure 10.1 is an example of an A letter.

Now that you have read the A letter, look at the B letter and see how some of the detail is replaced with more general statements (figure 10.2).

As you can see, the B letter is more generic and less exuberant than the A letter. What differentiates the C letter (figure 10.3) from the two previous references is its lengths. Short letters of recommendation are a signal to prospective employers that you did not have much good to say. When you come across letters of this type, you may want to investigate the bearer's background further before you hire him or her.

THE GROUP LETTER

These are the sorts of letters that nonwriters find the most difficult. When you need to write a letter of this type, approach your task in a way other

The A Letter of Reference

Dear (ask your employee whose name they would like here),

It is my pleasure to recommend Miss Allison Jayce for the position of social studies teacher at your school. I have worked with Allison for four years, and during that time I have noticed the following things about her:

A) She takes her teaching seriously and constantly reflects on how to stretch herself professionally.

B) She is aware of the school as a community and regularly contributes to school-wide activities outside the classroom.

C) She has assumed several leadership roles, including facilitator of the curriculum committee.

In short, Allison is a consummate professional and an example to her colleagues. I routinely receive positive comments about her contributions to her students' lives and have enjoyed working with her. She will be a fine addition in any capacity to your staff. Should you have any specific questions, I urge you to contact me at (330) 965-9421.

Sincerely,

Principal

Figure 10.1. The A Letter of Reference

The B Letter of Reference

To Whom It May Concern,

The purpose of this letter is to recommend Miss Allison Jayce for a
teaching position at your school. I have worked with Allison for four
years. During that time she has made several positive contributions to our
school, including the coordination of several assemblies and serving as a
member of our curriculum committee. She will be a stable addition to
your staff and community. It would be my pleasure to answer any
questions you have about her. You may contact me at (330) 965-9421.

Sincerely,

Principal

Figure 10.2.   The B Letter of Reference

than sitting before a blank screen or pad of paper. Reframe the writing
process in your mind into three distinct parts: prewriting, the hook, and
the sunset.

Prewriting is a process that does not necessarily require a writing
utensil. Prewriting for many authors (including this one) is the part
where you are thinking in your mind about the main ideas of what you
want to get across. The best time to involve yourself in this kind of
mental work is when you are relaxed. You can engage in prewriting
when you are driving your car, watching the final four during March
Madness, or working on your hobby. The magic of prewriting is that it
is a cerebral activity that you sort of focus on then forget about for a few
minutes then go back to and refocus on. You want to give your mind
these shifts in focus because prewriting is about deciding what is important to say. Prewriting is not about finding large vocabulary words
that make you sound important. Prewriting is not about sounding like

The C Letter of Reference

To Whom It May Concern,

The purpose of this letter is to serve as a reference for Miss Allison Jayce. I have worked with Allison for four years. Her primary responsibility has been teaching 6th grade. She is a member of a sixth-grade team consisting of three teachers responsible for our sixth-grade students. She has also been a member of the school improvement team. Should you have any specific questions, I urge you to contact me at (330) 965-9421.

Sincerely,

Principal

Figure 10.3. The C Letter of Reference

1. **Prewriting**

2. **Connecting ideas**

3. **Editing**

Figure 10.4. The Writing Process

Prewriting Questions

- What are the three most important things I want my readers to know?

- What are the supporting facts I want my readers to know?

- How do I want my readers to feel when they have finished reading my letter?

- Do I need to sound formal and professional in my writing, or less stiff and more casual?

Figure 10.5. Prewriting Questions

a school official. Prewriting is a method of solidifying ideas in your head about what you want to say in a way that makes sense to you. To illustrate how the prewriting process works, imagine that you are the newly hired principal of your alma mater, Boardman High School. While you were a student at Boardman, your parents were active community members. They have since moved away and you have only recently returned to your hometown. With these details in mind, look at the questions you can use when engaging in the prewriting process (figure 10.5).

The answers to these questions might be something like what is demonstrated in figure 10.6.

THE HOOK

The next part of prewriting is to think about how you are going to open your letter. Because this is a letter to a group of people, you can consider it as something akin to an essay. There are many different and specific functions of group letters; figure 10.7 is a general list of kinds of letters that belong to this genre.

1. My three most important things:

    a. I want my readers to see I am a product of our community.

    b. I want readers to see that I am also no longer the teenager that they might remember.

    c. I want readers to see that I am supportive of our faculty.

2. My supporting facts:

    a. I have solid professional credentials.

    b. I am a family man, with a wife who is a teacher.

    c. I intend to stay in this community for a long time.

    d. I want my readers to feel confident in my commitment to this school and excited about the new leadership team.

    e. I think I need to sound formal in some places, but familiar and casual in others.

Figure 10.6. Examples of Answers to Prewriting Questions

What distinguishes effective and interesting group letters from the same old memos churned out from the principal's office is the "hook" at the beginning. A hook is a paragraph that captures the reader's interest with something that he or she can relate to. Effective hooks do not begin with trite phrases like, "It was a dark and stormy night" or "As we consider education for the new millennium." When readers find these obvious and worn-out hooks, they lose interest immediately in what you have to say.

To find a good hook, go back to the three things you decided were the most important for your reader to know and then think of an event you have experienced related to those things. This will form the basis of your

Specific Kinds of Group Letters

1. Welcome back to school for parents and families to be sent a month before school starts)

2. Welcome back to school for teachers and staff (to be sent to employees a month before their report date)

3. Good-bye for the school year and welcome to summer for parents and families

4. End of the year good-bye and closing procedures for employees

5. Setting goals for the new year for parents and families

6. Setting goals for the new year for staff

7. Celebrating the profession of teaching for parents and families

8. Celebrating the profession of teaching for staff

9. Recognizing and celebrating the work of support staff for parents and faculty

10. Why reading is important for the community

11. Why reading should be an important part of any classroom for staff

12. Response to a local or national tragedy for community

13. Response to a local or national tragedy for staff

14. Explaining standardized testing and why it is important for parents and families

15. Explaining standardized testing in terms of your school's role to staff

Figure 10.7.   Specific Kinds of Group Letters

hook. This is still what you do while you are prewriting, which means you are churning these things over while driving, doing laundry, or exercising. A good hook is not pretentious and instantly relatable. Hooks are meant to make you think and help to open up an essay or letter to clarify your point.

If you need more inspiration to find good hooks, think about Andy Rooney, the famous writer for *Sixty Minutes*. How does he start his three-minute monologue every Sunday? By saying, "Have you ever noticed while standing in line . . ." or "The other day I was brushing my teeth and it occurred to . . ." This approach to opening a letter or essay with a small thing that everyone can relate to is the same technique that millionaire comedian Jerry Seinfeld and world-famous author Garrison Keillor use.

Are you still searching for the right hook? The last, most important hint concerning inspiration is to *write what you know.* Go back and read the stories at the beginning of each chapter in this book. Did you enjoy them? Were you able to sympathize with what some of the people were going through? Did you feel in some ways that you were listening to someone *real* telling you the sometimes ugly truth about leadership? Did you cringe when you read about the teacher who is a big shot or roll your eyes when you saw the description of the movie coach? If so, you experienced the power of a hook. You, like many other storytellers, can offer an insight or lesson by starting your letter with a simple hook in the form of a story that everyone can relate to.

At this point, go back to thinking about how you are the newly appointed principal of Boardman High School. You have figured out the answers to your prewriting questions and you have thought about a hook that is relevant to your message. For purposes of this discussion, let's say that you decided the hook you might like to use is a story about what it was like to walk the halls of your alma mater early one morning, right after you were awarded the job.

Now the fun begins, it is time to move to step three, where you connect the ideas together. Go to your computer or blank tablet and diagram out your letter. Much in the same way you diagram a play for a game, you outline what you think you might put in this letter. Figure 10.8 is a diagram of the letter of introduction that takes into account what the principal decided from the prewriting session described in figure 10.5.

THE SUNSET

At the bottom of the diagram in figure 10.8, you probably noticed the word "sunset" in parentheses. A sunset is the way to describe how to end a letter or essay in which you tie everything back to the beginning.

Diagram of the Group Letter

(Hook)   I was walking down the halls of Boardman High's social studies wing

thinking about my senior civics teacher, Mrs. Hill…

(Important thing)   I am a product of our community.

(Important thing)   I am no longer the teenager that they might remember.

(Supporting fact)   I have solid professional credentials.

(Supporting fact)   I am a family man with a wife who is a teacher and have a

son who will attend this high school in two years.

(Supporting fact)   I intend to stay in this community for a long time.

(How readers should feel) I am supportive of our faculty.

(How readers should feel) My commitment to this school is long term and

excited about the new leadership team.

(Sunset) Walking into my office and sitting down to write this letter.

Figure 10.8.   Diagram of the Group Letter

Because this letter begins with reflections of walking the halls of a cherished school, it makes sense that it would end with the returning graduate now a professional adult and leader walking into his new office and new position as principal. An essay is not complete without a sunset. Not all endings are sunsets either. When you brainstorm sunsets, think of the story you started to tell at the beginning of your letter, then look for ways to end your message by weaving the original hook back into the context of the bigger message.

EDITING

Editing is the last and most important phase in writing a letter. The first editing step after framing your rough draft is to put your letter away. Take a break from your brain work: Go have a beverage, watch a ball game, or go shopping. If you do not give your mind a rest from your work, you will not be able catch as many errors in syntax, context, and grammar. Your mental break should be an hour at least, but it is perfectly appropriate for it to last several days.

After resting your mind, the proper way to approach editing is to grab a pen just like your English teacher used to do and grade your paper. Read your letter out loud and listen for grammatical errors. Check for spelling errors. After you have notated the errors found in your first read, read your work out loud again. As you are listening to yourself read, think about how your intended audience would receive your message. Are you using words that are appropriate to their context? Do you sound too preachy? Does your letter sound condescending? Make changes according to these questions.

When you have completed all of your edits, you can do one of two things. You can call it your final copy and hand it over to whoever prints your letters for the masses. Or, you can find a trusted friend, teacher, or layman to read your letter and give you their suggestions. Running your letters past someone else is not always necessary, but an outsider's perspective always help buff away any little glitches you may have forgotten.

If you have followed the writing steps outlined earlier when considering your introductory letter to the Boardman High School community, you might end up with a letter that looks like the one in figure 10.9.

When considering the letter in figure 10.9, the structure is simple: hook, information, sunset. That is all one needs. Can you find the sunset? As you can see, it is not lengthy. The one sentence that alludes to the principal's pride at being a Boardman Tiger *again* is what ties the conclusion back to the original statement that this principal is an alumnus.

To see the recipe of hook, information, and sunset in another context, consider the letter in figure 10.10 written by a principal to encourage families to read together.

Dear Parents and Friends of Boardman High,

Last night, I was walking down the halls of Boardman High, looking at the newly decorated bulletin boards in the social studies wing. Even though it was past dinner-time, there were teachers diligently setting up their classroom and organizing their lessons for the upcoming fall semester.

I could not help but feel an incredible sense of pride as I reflected on the level of commitment that binds our family of educators and staff together. The folks here are serious about challenging students and helping them to develop thoughtful academic and professional goals that will last a lifetime. I can say this not only because of what I have observed as the new principal during the last month, but because I was one of the students who experienced this staff's dedication firsthand. It was Mrs. Kyle who first inspired me to want to become a teacher. And it was Mr. Price, our recently retired student government sponsor, who taught me the value of giving back to the community. But perhaps the person who taught me the most about what it means to be a Boardman Tiger was Coach Harrell. When I was disappointed that I did not receive a college basketball scholarship, he helped me to understand that there were other more important challenges in the world.

Throughout my college experience at Purdue and teaching adventures in Chicago, I would visit the Boardman family whenever I returned here to my hometown. While I am no longer the boy who left Boardman in 1985, I am thrilled to return to this community as your principal. I am so very excited at the prospect of sharing this caring environment with my wife, also a teacher, and my son, who will attend Franklin Middle School this year.

As a 'sort of' new resident, I continue to be impressed with the Boardman neighborhood's commitment to supporting the achievements of Boardman students, be it through service learning projects, partnerships with local businesses such as the Crago veterinary clinic, or academic decathlon competitions.

The presemester buzz on campus obviously demonstrates our staff's excitement about our students' return to school. We have been working nonstop to make the August 25th opening day of school as smooth as possible for you and your child. Attached in this packet, you will find registration and textbook information along with your child's schedule. Lastly, there is a calendar that outlines the dates and times of our parent and community meetings. You will notice that we are having a community ice cream social at the Pulaski Club on Saturday, August 23 from 4-7 pm. Please consider attending this family event so that we can meet in person. If you have any questions before that time feel free to call me at 330 672 0004. It feels great to be a Tiger again, and I look forward to seeing you.

Sincerely,
The principal

Figure 10.9. Example of a Letter Written Using the Hook, Information, and the Sunset

Dear Parents,

Quick . . . close your eyes and try to remember the first book you ever came across. Was it Frank Baum's *The Wizard of Oz*? Maybe it was *Harold and the Purple Crayon*. Were you a Nancy Drew fan, or did you like adventure books like *Call of the Wild*? Whatever your favorite story was, when you closed your eyes and reflected on your very first book, odds are that you smiled. That smile is the result of all the feelings of wonder and curiosity and safety that make childhood a delicious place.

Childhood is richer when there are adventures to be had inside a book. By empowering your children to read, you are encouraging them to stretch themselves. There are essentially two kinds of readers: those who travel through time and space by way of their literate behavior, and those who engage in reading behavior only when there is a cereal box around. Do not let your child become such a passive reader!

There are tons of research demonstrating the lifelong value of engaging children in reading behaviors. Children who regularly engage in literate behavior are in general more successful in school and in life than children who do not engage in reading behavior. If you want your child to develop into the former group rather than the latter, consider these tips:
- Subscribe to a child's magazine such as *Highlights*, along with *National Geographic* so that your child is exposed to both.
- Get your child a library card and take them regularly to the public library.
- Keep a basket in the bathroom full of reading material.
- Read together with your child every day; if they can independently read, share a book with them and discuss the chapters together as you go through them.

Perhaps the most important tip to help your child become a lifelong reader is to model a love of reading yourself. You don't have to read dry, boring, novels to be a reader. And your children should know that good readers don't always read difficult material. Reading is still an entertaining endeavor; perhaps the best place to remind ourselves and teach our children that lesson is to find out first childhood book and share it with the ones you love. As for me, I am going to dust off Dr. Seuss' *Oh, the Places You'll Go* and share it with my seventeen-year-old senior over pizza tonight.

Happy reading,
The principal

Figure 10.10. Example 2 of a Letter Written Using the Hook, Information, and the Sunset

THE LETTER BREAKING BAD NEWS

From time to time in your career, you will have the unpleasant task of writing a letter to your community and/or teaching staff that informs them of unpleasant news. When this is the case, you should consider a different letter recipe. Instead of hook, information, sunset, your format should be information, suggestions, condolences. Here is how a letter such as this might look after the death of three students involved in an automobile accident (figure 10.11).

THE NEWSLETTER TO STAFF

One of the best ways to communicate consistently with your staff is to publish a weekly, or biweekly, newsletter to all of your teachers and support staff. This is a great tool to celebrate accomplishments, increase a sense of community, and consistently reinforce the vision. If you need a reminder of why you need to reinforce your visions and expectations, go back and

---

Dear Parents,

It is with a heavy heart that I must inform you that our school community lost three of its students over the weekend after a football game at Chaney High School. Seniors Casey Marin, Sarah Long, and Andrew Manson were involved in a fatal automobile accident on the icy roads at approximately 11p.m. I have been in contact with all three families and have been informed that funeral arrangements for these students will be announced in the local paper this Wednesday. If your family or child wishes to attend the services, we of course understand and request that you simply inform our attendance office by phone at 330 672 0500 or by way of a note. We would also like to encourage you to talk about this incident with your child. We have assembled our school's crisis team to provide private counseling for any student who requests assistance during this difficult time. Our student government is meeting this week to consider what options our student body has in terms of remembering and celebrating the contributions of their classmates. I know I represent the entire school staff when I share with you our deepest sympathies and a commitment to help our school family endure and recover from this tragedy. If you have any questions or concerns, I urge you to contact me at 330 672 0020.

Sincerely,
The principal

Figure 10.11.   Example of a Letter Written Using Information, Suggestions, and Condolences

read chapter 2. The disadvantage of doing a newsletter is that you have to keep up with it. You have to be consistent. If you are not, people will notice; it will seem to you that just as you have gotten your employees in a place where they feel validated and excited, you will lose credibility because you might have talked up a newsletter but lacked the follow-through to keep it going. If you do decide to have a weekly newsletter for your staff, consider the suggestions in figure 10.12.

Things to Put in a Staff Newsletter

- Staff birthdays

- Kudos for good deeds

- Highlights of staff's family members

- Relevant and important district meeting dates

- Quote of the day

- Recommendations for books to read

- Outline of relevant news items in local or national paper or television

- Highlights of student accomplishments

- Schedule of what the cafeteria is serving for the week

- Requests for feedback from staff regarding a specific question. (The questions can be fun or serious.)

- Reminder of Board of Education meetings, day and time

- Reminder of how to reinforce tardy policy or student dress code

- Kudos to athletic team for a game well played or won

- Notifications of sales at local teacher supply or craft stores

Figure 10.12.   Things to Put in a Staff Newsletter

THE LETTER OF REPRIMAND

Chapter 5 presented a discussion of what to do when things get ugly in terms of how to handle a disciplinary meeting and how to document events. This section is designed to demonstrate what a letter of reprimand looks like. When you write a letter of reprimand, the most important thing to remember is that you must be accurate in both your facts and the governing board polices related to the offense described by the employee. The recipe for a letter of this type is as follows: Statement of facts including dates and times of employee's misconduct, statement of governing board policies breached, statement of punishment, a statement informing reader that you look forward to continued collaboration. Figure 10.13 is an example of a letter of reprimand for an employee who used the "F word" when addressing his students after being directed on two separate occasions to refrain from this behavior.

This is the type of letter that you will need to deliver and review in person with the employee who is receiving it. A meeting for reviewing this letter should be conducted in the same manner that was described in the Plan of Improvement section of chapter 5. The most important aspect of a review meeting such as this is to remember that you must have your facts correct, and a wise principal would consider running the entire scenario past the personnel director to ensure that district policies are followed.

THE LETTER OF CONFIRMATION

What makes a letter of confirmation useful is that it does not have the brevity a formal letter of reprimand has, yet it can raise the level of an employee's concern. Essentially, the recipe is the same as for the letter of reprimand except this letter focuses on communicating an expectation. While these letters are not placed in employee files, copies should be kept for your records. Letters of confirmation help to supplement the documentation necessary to ultimately generate a letter of reprimand. The purpose is essentially to confirm you have informed an employee of a particular policy, practice, or expectation regarding his or her performance. Figure 10.14 is an example of this type of letter, written for a teacher who insists on missing faculty meetings because she chooses to

March 25, 2004
To: Mr. Zach
From: Principal Gramuffle
Re: Events of 3rd hour class on March 21, 2004

The purpose of this letter is to inform you that on March 21st, a student informed me that you used inappropriate language while addressing a student during your third hour class. After investigating this charge with your colleagues and with other students, I have come to the conclusion that it is true. On January 14 of 2003, you and I met informally to discuss a similar charge and at that point you were directed not to use inappropriate language with your students. We met again on March 1, 2004, to discuss another incident in which you again used inappropriate language. Because this is the third time in which you have disregarded my request, I must inform you that you are in violation of Marsh District Governing Board Policy MDGBP10-11165 that states: "Teachers will conduct themselves is professional and ethical manner at all times during the school day."

Because you continue to violate this policy, these three incidences will be reflected in your annual performance evaluation. Additionally, a copy of this letter will be placed in your file for a period of two years. My expectation for your continued success is that you will terminate this behavior. I look forward to collaborating with you in the future.

Figure 10.13. Example of a Letter of Reprimand

take her son to doctor appointments and yet refuses to submit a note from her son's physician verifying her visits.

Again, meeting with the recipient of this letter is necessary in order to review in person your concerns. When you host this meeting, use this letter as a tool to help your employee understand that you are serious about the issues raised in the letter and use it as a springboard for discussions about the issues outlined in the letter. Do not be surprised if your employee interrupts the meeting to ask for a union representative. He or she may not understand that this is a letter of confirmation rather than a letter of reprimand. Remember that this process can produce anxiety in your employee and that is not necessarily a bad thing.

Date: September 15, 2004
To: Jennifer Laird
From: Carla Smith
Re: Faculty meetings

The purpose of this letter to confirm that you have been informed that Hand
District Governing Board Policy HDGBP112260 requires "…teachers to
regularly attend faculty meetings in order to collaborate with their colleagues
and engage in staff development opportunities." Thus far this year you have
missed a total of four meetings, each time explaining to me on the day following
the meeting that you were taking your son to the doctor. I have asked you
repeatedly to provide me with a note from your son's doctor confirming the
reason for your absence. I am taking this opportunity to ask again that you
provide me this note by September 25, 2004. I look forward to collaborating
with you in this matter.

Figure 10.14. Example of a Letter of Confirmation

CHAPTER 10 INSTANT REPLAY:
THE LETTER ARSENAL

1. Write your letters of reference ahead of time and keep them ready on your computer in order to save time when people ask you for recommendations.
2. Be timely in providing letters of recommendation for those who ask.
3. Edit, edit, edit. Make sure your letters are professional and free of grammatical and spelling errors.
4. Engage in prewriting as a way to brainstorm your letters to large groups.
5. Diagram your letters in order to see if you have all the important aspects and supporting facts and are conscious of how you want your readers to feel.
6. Use your own voice; don't try to sound like a principal all the time.
7. When you have downtime, brainstorm a list of letter topics for staff and community that you can write each month.
8. When you come across essays or newsletters that you enjoy, save them in a writing file to refer to when you need inspiration.
9. Ask you principal colleagues to share ideas for letters that they have used.
10. Be correct in your facts when writing.

11

SECRETS
OF
CHAMPIONS

Paradise Valley High School's auditorium was a sea of red and white. Every person in this packed room had on the school colors in one form or another. School spirit was represented in ways that ranged from the red yarn tied around girls' ponytails to the "PV" letters painted on the cheeks of band members.

"I heart PV" candy wrappers were spilling out of garbage cans in the lobby. Teachers, decked out in PV pride sweatshirts, sat patiently in their assigned sections in the audience waiting for the assembly to begin.

Paradise Valley's newest faculty member, Amber Smith, was helping the head of the counseling department, Julie Farnam, direct traffic through the aisles in the back of the auditorium. Amber respected Julie: She was an effective department chair and a good counselor and really cared about the students. In between shuffling students, the two women shared their observation that the activities of the past few days had seemed to energize the school. Even the more reserved and senior faculty members were enjoying Spirit Week at PV High. Amber looked around the auditorium for the administrative team. She was trying to start thinking like an administrator because she was working toward her master's degree in educational leadership. So now it was natural for her to try and think about how her supervisors handled things like campus events and meetings.

She looked around to see who was doing what. The athletic director was by the orchestra pit and the assistant principals had stationed themselves by the north and south exits. But where was the principal? Just as she tried to ask Julie, "Where's Gary?" the lights went down and students began to shush each other.

The curtains opened on the stage to reveal the student body president standing behind a microphone lit by a single hard spotlight. The audience reacted to his presence with the usual teenage pomp and circumstance that included "woofing" noises and whistles. The president, in turn, returned the ritualistic greeting by screaming into the microphone, "What's up Peeee Veeee!" The phrase was more a proclamation than a question.

The crowd cheered, the president bantered some more about school spirit and proceeded to welcome the audience to the spirit assembly to celebrate "unity, diversity, and the culture of our Paradise Valley High School community."

He then introduced the Girls' Senior Dance Team who began performing to another round of whistles and cheers. This was followed by a slide show highlighting students' achievements. As the pictures of various teachers and students were flashed on the screen, the crowd reacted by cheering a little louder or barking. Then there was a performance by a local jazz fusion band. People began clapping and dancing in the aisles as if they were in a night club. The band closed its set by offering a few words about the importance of unity and honoring diversity. These oh-so-cool high school students cheered even louder at the lead singer's message. Next, it was time for another slide show honoring student work in the community.

In the midst of the cheering, Amber thought to herself that this was not just a standard assembly. Kids always get excited over athletic events and cheerleaders, but this time it was different. The buzz in the crowd really was about school pride and a celebration of differences. There had been so many creative things in the past week at school that involved students as well as teachers. The planning committee had even created integrated lesson plans that all teachers could use in their classrooms. There had been ideas and kudos all over the staff newsletter and in the teachers' lounge. The halls were decorated with themed posters and slogans. And yes, at this moment, in the midst of the cheering and singing, this school felt like a family. Amber noticed that there also seemed to be a lack of discipline problems at the assembly. But where was Gary Damore? Amber remembered that he had facilitated the work of the planning team for this weeklong event; it made no sense that he was not there. This was exactly his kind of thing. Gary was creative and loved kids, he had to be somewhere in that auditorium.

Just as Amber tried to look behind her for Gary, the opening notes to the song "I'll Take You There" slithered through the auditorium and the lights on stage revealed a sort of conga line of students holding hands and dancing to the beat of the Staples Singers' 1972 classic. Amber's attention was back on the stage. She was so focused, she did not notice that she was dancing out of her chair. Julie leaned over and said, "I bet you ten bucks these kids don't even know who sings this song. They probably have never even heard of the Staples Singers and look at them; they are having a blast." Amber replied, "Yeah, you either feel this music or you don't. It looks to me like everyone is feeling it."

The students on stage kept coming out in a line dancing to the lyrics and holding hands as a sign of unity. Just as the song found its chorus, the audience screamed even louder. There on stage, in the midst of the kids grooving to the music, was Gary Damore, Paradise Valley's beloved principal. To everyone's delight, this normally conservative father figure was feeling the music too. His daily uniform of perfect grey suits, starched white shirts, and silk red ties had been replaced with jeans and a tie-dyed shirt. Best of all, the man had wrapped a bandanna around his middle-aged head.

It was clear he was having a good time, and he was not the only one savoring the moment. The audience truly got a kick out of seeing this charismatic principal out of his element and still cutting loose with the kids. It was just the perfect school moment in a Norman-Rockwell–Americana sort of way. Kids were now flooding out into the aisle, not in chaos, but wrapped up in the joy of the spectacle. And the staff was right there with them, dancing and clapping and cheering. Amber thought to herself, "This is the kind of stuff they talk about in my graduate classes. This is what building a vision looks like. Up there is the kind of leader I want to be when I grow up."

STARTING PLAYERS VERSUS HALL-OF-FAMERS

The truth is that most folks who are willing to get the correct credentials and find a school community in which they *fit* can become principals. However, there is a huge difference between being a principal and being an inspiration. And just like scouts are able to spot talent early on in an athlete's career, it is possible to spot talent in an administrative career and it's even easier to spot the phenoms. In the words of one colleague, "Cream always rises to the top." This chapter is different than the earlier ones in that the unifying theme is simply a patchwork of ideas presented as bullets of advice to help you understand how the really great principals go about their jobs. These principals, like Gary Damore, are leaders in every essence of the word, particularly in terms of their potential and ability to inspire others. When you review these insights, reflect on how they can help you this year and in the years to come.

THE PRINCIPAL AS READER

Being the educational leader of a school is one thing. Being a literacy apostle for the people you serve is quite another. The ability to touch another's life by way of the gift of a book is not such a difficult goal to aspire to. However, it does require you to reflect on your own rolodex of literary works that you have enjoyed. Being aware of this rolodex is a small discipline that is akin to recommending a movie to a friend. After you see a particular movie, you might think about where it was filmed and then realize your friend would like the scenery, drama, or the great performance of the hunky star.

If you can't remember the last book or poem you have read, take heart. There are places all over the Internet to help whet your appetite for a book or to remind you of good ones you have delved into before. Do you want to check out a few of the 100 greatest poems ever written? Go to www.poetry.com/greatestpoems/list.asp.

Perhaps you would like to see what the Modern Library lists as the 100 best novels. Then surf to www.randomhouse.com/modernlibrary/100bestnovels.html.

If you enjoy nonfiction, check another Random House website: www.randomhouse.com/modernlibrary/100bestnonfiction.html.

Do you remember the first time you read Shirley Jackson's creepy short story called "The Lottery"? If you would like to explore other short stories from the masters of this genre go to http://ee.1asphost.com/shortstoryclassics/index.html. And Billy Collins, former poet laureate for the United States, has compiled a list of 180 poems (one a day for the entire school year) he believes are interesting for students. They are at this website: www.loc.gov/poetry/180. If you are looking for ways to help those around you beef up their own rolodex of great literary works, consider putting up a bulletin board in a central place where you post the lists offered on these websites. Schools are not the only places where reading becomes part of the culture. One Ohio-based public relations firm has a bookcase in the employees' rest rooms filled with books that coworkers share. A whiteboard on the wall lists the books and who brought them in so that borrowers can ask donors about them. Another whiteboard contains a current book title and people are free to make reviewers' comments as they come and go throughout the day. You could do the same thing at your place of work. Make your own "lounge library" or put up a poem on a whiteboard and invite passersby to graffiti their impressions of the work. Running conversations about literature do not always have to take place in person. It can be a real morale boost to see conversations evolve on a community whiteboard.

Another idea to beef up your literary rolodex is to sponsor a book club or series of book talks. You can have a book club for your teachers and a separate one for your community. Have an initial meeting and ask the attendees what sort of book they would like to read. Give them themes to choose from: classics, Oprah's book lists, or even something from the websites previously mentioned. Maybe there is a book you have always wanted to read but never got around to it. Perhaps you enjoyed a movie and would like to see how closely it followed the book. Below is a list of books to get your brain working that would be appropriate for you to read with your faculty. For books that are published from small publishing firms, the author included contact information on the list. Also, do not be disheartened if these books are out of print; it is still quite easy to find an out-of-print book on the Internet (figure 11.1).

If you are interested in looking for a list of books for a community book club remember that the theme you select can help drive an agenda. So you might want to pick the book yourself depending on a particular agenda you may have. For example, let's say that you are interested in talking to your community about school safety issues. You might select Gavin De Becker's book *The Gift of Fear.* Or your first agenda item with your community might be to just get to know them. In that case you might pick a lighter subject such as Benjamin Hoff's book *The Tao of Pooh*. Consider the list of suggestions in figure 11.2 for community book talks.

Find group consensus on a book choice and agree on a time to meet again and discuss the first three chapters, or the first half of the book, or even the entire book. Then when you meet again (preferably over coffee or adult beverages, or bowling), talk about what you liked and what

Great Books for Faculty Book Clubs

1. *It's about Time,* by Jim Bruno

2. *Bilingualism in Education* by Cummins and Swain

3. *Joystick Nation* by J.C. Herz

4. *Principals and Standards for School Mathematics,* by the NCTM 1 800 253 7566

5. *The Bell Curve* by Hernstein and Murray

6. *Conflict of Interests: The Politics of American Education* by Joel Spring

7. *The Differentiated Classroom* by Carol Ann Tomlinson 1 800 933 2723 (ASCD)

8. *Book Buddies* by Francine Johnson, et al.

9. *A Teacher's Guide to Standardized Reading Tests* by Lucy Calkins Heinman
   Publications www.heinemann.com

10. *Making Standards Work* by Reeves -www.testdoctor.com 1-800-THINK-99

11. *Enhancing Professional Practice* by Charlotte Danielson (ASCD) 703 549 9110

12. *ITI the Model: Integrated Thematic Instruction* by Susan Kovalik 206 630 6908

13. *Preparing Instructional Objectives* by Robert Mager 1 800 558 4CEP

14. *Reading Instruction That Works* by Micheal Pressley

15. *The First Days of School* by Harry Wong

Figure 11.1. Great Books for Faculty Book Clubs

you didn't. Books are more delicious when you can share them with someone. Another idea is to revisit a childhood book and share the adventure with friends or colleagues through your adult lenses. Dr. Seuss is famous for weaving very adult topics in whimsical children's stories. Grab *Green Eggs and Ham* and have a night out with your community to talk about it.

Books are wonderful, intimate, and very symbolic gifts. If you have a friend or colleague who needs a little happy pick-me-up, consider giving these titles offered in figure 11.3.

Great Books for Community Book Clubs

1. *The Gift of Fear* by Gavin Debecker

2. *Women, Race and Class* by Angela Davis

3. *The Fight in the Fields: Cesar Chavez and the Farm Workers Movement* by Susan Ferriss

4. *The Fountainhead* by Ayn Rand

5. *Undaunted Courage* by Stephen Ambrose

6. *Walden* by Henry David Thoreau

7. *Les Miserables* by Victor Hugo

8. *White Jacket* by John Steinbeck

9. *Mountain Interval* by Robert Frost .

10. *Siddhartha: An Indian Tale* by Hess, Neugroshel, and Freedman

11. *Ten Poems to Change Your Life* by Houseden

12. *A Patriot's Handbook* by Caroline Kennedy

13. *How Reading Changed My Life* by Anna Quindlen

14. *The Bell Jar* by Sylvia Plath

15. *Growing Up Digital* by Don Tapscott

Figure 11.2. Great Books for Community Book Clubs

Books say a lot about who we are. When they sit on the shelves of our offices, they tell the observer what we appreciate, what we admire, and what we enjoy. Have you seen a great movie lately with a friend or a loved one? Was a book referenced in the movie? Terrific, you have an automatic gift idea: Go get that book and read it. Better yet, give it to your movie companion. This author discovered a poet named A. E. Houseman because in the movie *Out of Africa*, Meryl Streep (playing adventuress Karin Von Blixen) read the poem "To an Athlete Dying Young" in a heart-wrenching funeral scene. Finding this poem was not

Great Books to Give as Gifts

1. *American Sphinx* by Joseph Ellis

2. *Iacocca : An Autobiography* by Lee Iacocca, William Novak;

3. *Jack: Straight from the Gut* by Jack Welch

4. *The Seven Secrets of Successful Coaches* by Jeff Janssen

5. *They Shoot Coaches, Don't They? UCLA and the NCAA since John Wooden* by Mark Heisler

6. *Lou Holtz & Notre Dame: Deception under the Golden Dome* by Don Yaeger

7. *Women Who Run with the Wolves* by Clarissa Estes

8. *Gift from the Sea* by Anne Morrow Lindbergh

9. *I Know Why the Caged Bird Sings* by Maya Angelou

10. *Out of Africa* by Issac Dinesen

11. *Reviving Ophelia* by Mary Pipher

12. *Other People's Children* by Lisa Delpit

13. *The Tao of Pooh* by Benjamin Hoff

14. *The Te of Piglet* by Benjamin Hoff

15. Any book by Dr. Seuss (for any age recipient)

16. *To Kill a Mockingbird* by Harper Lee

Figure 11.3. Great Books to Give as Gifts

difficult at all, thanks to the Internet. Some movies are only based on one of a series of books. If you saw *Divine Secrets of the Ya-Ya Sisterhood* and liked it, go get Rebecca Wells's prequel novel, *Little Altars Everywhere*.

What if you feel like you never have time to read? There are plenty of books on tape. Nothing is more decadent than to have a book read to you. If you have a willing reading partner, road trips are made all the more entertaining by sharing a book with whoever rides shotgun.

Any book by short story humorist David Sedaris is a great choice for road trip reading. Another colleague of mine loves to go to estate sales with his wife every Saturday. In between sales, his wife reads aloud in the car the science fiction and fantasy books of Diane Gabaldon.

If you are looking for other ways to find a book to be interested in, figure out where National Public Radio is located on your local radio dial. This station sponsors several wonderful programs on the weekend dedicated to talking about books or reference books, music, and other efforts in the area of liberal arts and culture. Known authors, such as David Sedaris, often contribute stories. In partnership with National Public Radio, Borders bookstore has a section that displays the books and music referenced each week on National Public Radio.

The last thing to recognize when thinking about the power of the right book at the right time is to realize that you need to have some sense of the person to whom you will be giving a book. Receiving a book as a gift does not (and often should not) have to feel like homework. Some people who are not readers may enjoy a book that is not text-rich, but will have information valuable to them. Or you may be able to provide them with books that serve as conduits for reading other books. A fine example of this paradox lies in the never-ending search for a birthday present for my best friend, the nonreader. This friend of mine would rather coach basketball and buy Nike shoes than read. She loves her Nike tennis shoes so much that she has stock in the Nike Corporation. So when *Nike, Yesterday and Today: A Fulcrum of Nike History* by Ibani Ibani was on the shelves at the local bookstore, the birthday present dilemma was instantly solved. This Nike fashionista happily devoured her book because it was a complete history of every shoe Nike ever made.

Furthermore, this book inspired her to read *Nike Culture* by Stephen Papson and Robert Founder. Now, she gives both books to all of the members of her varsity basketball team. Is this the same as giving teenagers Walt Whitman? No. But there are now teenagers reading a genre of books that they did not know existed. The more one reads, the more literate he or she tends to become. And the greater one's literacy skills, the more likely he or she will continue to read. Ultimately, that reader will spread the word about the latest treasure he or she discovered or heard about. This circle of influence from one literacy apostle to another—to a whole community and generation of readers—is the magic that the right book at the right time can manifest. If you are curious as to how the author comprised the lists of "great books" they are strictly out of her own experiences with the book clubs she was involved with while a principal and are also books she uses currently in the leadership courses she teaches.

THE PRINCIPAL'S TO-DO LIST

The secret to staying organized as a principal is to make, follow, and revise to-do lists for every month of the year. Figures 11.4 through 11.15 offer a skeleton of each month that contains the bare bones of what you should be thinking about each month. In order to use them in the most efficient way, copy these lists and then pencil in your own additions. Then every year, update these lists with additions or deletions.

Things for August

• Finalize arrangements for welcome back in-service for teachers

• Check that all teaching supplies, furniture, and textbook orders have been filled

• Arrange dates for school pictures, Open House and parent-teacher conferences

• Meet with maintenance staff to ensure that grounds are ready for opening day

• Check in with faculty as they set up classrooms

• Go over opening day procedures with office staff

• Conduct welcome back in-service

• Write September community letter and staff letter

Figure 11.4. August To-Do List

Things for September

- Send September letters to parents and staff

- Calendar preobservation conferences, observations, and postconferences for fall semester

- Recruit new volunteers for school committees; host first meeting of the year for each committee

- Finalize plans and arrangements for Open House and parent-teacher conferences

- Begin classroom observations and write up evaluations

- Write October community letter and staff letter

- Send thank-you and kudos notes to staff

- Plan for nurses' appreciation day

Figure 11.5.   September To-Do List

Things for October

- Send October letters to parents and staff

- Conduct classroom observations and evaluation conferences

- Review last year's standardized test scores with staff

- Network with principal colleagues to reflect on the year and set goals

- In-service staff on yearlong curriculum plan to improve standardized scores

- Write November community letter and staff letter

- Send thank-you and kudos notes to staff

Figure 11.6.   October To-Do List

Things for November

- Send November letters to parents and staff

- Conduct classroom observations and evaluation conferences

- In-service staff on yearlong curriculum plan to improve standardized scores

- Write December community letter and staff letter

- Send thank-you and kudos notes to staff

- Highlight school safety as an in-service for staff

- Prepare/plan fall semester award ceremony and recognitions

- Review fall semester and yearly budget, project needs

- Order supplies for spring semester

- Meet with Personnel Director to discuss possible employees who qualify for a plan of improvement or a nonrenewed contract

- Identify seniors who are failing, plan interventions and school support strategies such as Saturday school or peer tutoring

Figure 11.7. November To-Do List

Things for December

- Send December letters to parents and staff

- Conduct classroom observations and evaluation conferences

- Meet with staff individually for a midyear check-in

- Meet with administrative team to reflect on success/challenges from fall semester

- In-service staff on yearlong curriculum plan to improve standardized scores

- Write and send a memo to teachers outlining specific expectations for classroom activities for the last week before holiday break. (Do you really want everyone watching television the last day?)

- Write and distribute Happy Winter break community letter and staff letter

- Write January "Welcome Back" letter for community and staff

- Send holiday greeting cards to staff, parent volunteers, community businesses in your attendance zone

- Network with principal colleagues to reflect on the semester and wish happy holidays

Figure 11.8. December To-Do List

Things for January

- Send Welcome Back to the New Year letters to parents and staff

- Conduct classroom observations and evaluation conferences

- Write and send thank-you cards for holiday gifts you and/or the school received.

- In-service teachers on subject related to standardized testing

- Identify seniors who are in danger of failing and plan strategies to help them

- Review district procedures for submitting budget requests

- Calendar preobservation conferences, observations, and postconferences for spring semester

- Set goals for administrative team for the spring semester

- Create graduation committee

- Review end-of-the-year procedures

- Write February community letter and staff letter

Figure 11.9. January To-Do List

Things for February

- Send February letters to parents and staff

- Conduct classroom observations and evaluation conferences

- Network with principal colleagues to reflect on the year and set goals

- Write and send thank-you cards for holiday gifts you and/or the school received.

- In-service teachers on subject related to standardized testing

- Identify seniors who are in danger of failing and plan strategies to help them

- Review district procedures for submitting budget requests

- Calendar preobservation conferences, observations, and postconferences for spring semester

- Plan teacher and staff appreciation week

- Set goals for administrative team for the spring semester

- Create graduation committee

- Review end-of-the-year procedures

- Write March community letter and staff letter

- Send thank-you and kudos notes to staff

Figure 11.10. February To-Do List

Things for March

- Send March letters to parents and staff

- Review and make changes to student handbook; submit to printer

- Conduct classroom observations and evaluation conferences

- In-service teachers on subjects related to standardized testing

- Identify seniors who are in danger of failing and plan strategies to help them

- Review district procedures for submitting budget requests

- Calendar preobservation conferences, observations, and postconferences for spring semester

- Delegate, review, and conduct support staff evaluations

- Prioritize school budget for next year

- Prioritize campus site needs/improvements with maintenance staff

- Plan student end-of-year recognition program

- Plan end-of-year thank-you luncheon or event for school volunteers

- Finalize paperwork for employees on nonrenewals

- Write April community letter and staff letter

- Send thank-you and kudos notes to staff

Figure 11.11.   March To-Do List

Things for April

- Send April letters to parents and staff

- Conduct final classroom observations and evaluation conferences

- In-service teachers on subjects related to standardized testing

- Identify seniors who are in danger of failing and plan strategies to help them; contact parents for final reminders of student's situation

- Conduct meetings to inform employees of nonrenewal status

- Plan end-of-year activities for community (summer carnival, etc.)

- Prioritize campus needs/improvements for summer school with maintenance staff

- Announce Master Schedule for next year

- Identify staff vacancies for next year

- Plan kindergarten roundup

- Plan room changes for the following year

- Write May community letter and staff letter

- Network with principal colleagues to reflect on the year and set goals

- Send thank-you and kudos notes to staff

Figure 11.12.   April To-Do List

Things for May

- Send May letters to parents and staff

- In-service teachers on subjects related to end-of-the-year closing procedures

- Continue to identify seniors who are in danger of failing and plan strategies to help them; contact parents for final reminders of student's situation

- Conduct meetings to inform employees of nonrenewal status

- Finalize graduation ceremony

- Announce room changes for next year

- Continue to identify staff vacancies for next year

- Host kindergarten roundup

- Host end-of-year celebrations for teachers, community, and staff

- Write end-of-year community letter and staff letter

- Elicit from staff what improvements they would like to see in school organization: utilize their input if you agree. If you don't see their suggestions as doable, explain reasons why to staff

- Review current school calendar and revamp for next year

- Order supplies for next year

- Write end-of-school-year letter for community and staff

- Send thank-you and kudos notes to staff

Figure 11.13. May To-Do List

Things for June

- Send end-of-year letters to parents and staff

- Meet with administrative team to reflect on year's successes and challenges; set goals for next year

- Interview and hire applicants for posted staff and teaching positions

- Review and change monthly to-do list for next year

- Review fall site needs and improvements with your maintenance staff

- Write 'Welcome Back' letters for staff and community

- Review, change, and improve 'Welcome Back' packet for teachers and students

- Write thank-you and kudos notes to staff, parents, and businesses in the community

- Network with principal colleagues to reflect on the year and to set goals

- Finalize budget

Figure 11.14. June To-Do List

Things for July

- Disconnect from your job for as long as possible (one to two weeks)

- Set up your personal calendar as described in chapters 2 and 3

- Interview and hire applicants for posted staff and teaching positions

- Notify Director of Personnel if you are having problems filling a particular vacancy

- Review fall site needs and improvements with your maintenance staff

- Clean out your office; throw away outdated materials, books, and pamphlets

- Take your secretarial staff to lunch and schedule in your calendar three dates in the school year when you will have lunch brought in for them.

- Review your school's academic performance record and draft a plan to improve school's rating

- Identify, contact, and schedule in-service consultants

- Make and review purchase orders for fall books, furniture, and supplies

- Finalize school calendar for next year.

- Spend some quality time reflecting on last year's successes and challenges

- Set your own personal goals

Figure 11.15. July To-Do List

You also may want to identify for yourself things that you need to do every month. Here is a list that contains some items previously mentioned to get you started (figure 11.16).

REWARDING AND RECOGNIZING YOUR COLLEAGUES

The champions in the principalship realize that a school really is a team. As such, they seek to regularly reward those around them. You read in earlier chapters that positive reinforcement increases morale and buy-in. Do not forget it. Figure 11.17 is a list of ways to recognize the people who work so hard for you.

Things to Do Once a Month

- Lockdown drills and fire drills

- Recognize a staff member, teacher, and student publicly

- Eat lunch with an employee or student

- Host book talks or book clubs for community or faculty

- Host faculty meeting/in-services

- Write letters to the community

- Write a staff newsletter

- Network with your colleagues who are principals

- Network with community members

- Host a Participatory Management Team meeting

- Attend PTA/PTO meetings

- Decorate the teachers' lounge

- Make sure the staff rest rooms are maintained with extras like lotion, hairspray, and tissues

Figure 11.16. Once a Month To-Do List

Ways to Reward Staff

1. Hire or invite students in a cosmetology school to give staff manicures

2. Cook and/or serve the entire staff lunch or breakfast

3. Sincere, handwritten, and personalized notes

4. The gift of a book

5. Substitute-teach their class while they enjoy a break

6. Deliver a special surprise to every classroom (a flower or snack)

7. Leave a surprise for the staff to find at their desks (a snack or T-shirt)

8. Buy staff shirts to welcome everyone back for the fall. (Get the correct sizes; do not embarrass someone with a shirt that is too small or does not fit.)

9. Thank employees with a lottery ticket

10. Hire or invite masseuses to give quick shoulder and back rubs for folks at lunch. (Some will do this for free in exchange for advertising with your staff.)

11. Distribute disposable cameras on special days to staff and students (opening day, a school celebration). Host a slide show of different pictures along with treats.

12. Say "thank you" when it is warranted

Figure 11.17. Examples of Ways to Reward Staff

THE SECRETS OF CHAMPIONS

In the end, when considering the difference between good principals and legendary ones, a great deal comes down to the makeup of the individual. These qualities are often not concrete and absolutely innate. The list in figure 11.18 is neither subjective nor concrete but should serve as an adequate marker to help you identify the stellar principals in your life.

Things That Distinguish Great Principals from the Rest of the Team

1. They really care about people

2. They are not selfish or egocentric

3. They are just as likely to wipe down a lunch table as they are to sit in the dunk tank

4. They do good things when no one is watching

5. They read

6. They were and are good teachers

7. They believe that they are on a mission

8. They reflect regularly on their choices and behavior

9. They value doing what is right over being popular

10. They can laugh at themselves

11. They preserve their employees' dignity

12. They know their moral compass

13. They include and celebrate their school leadership team

14. They are creative and think outside the box

15. They take risks

16. They put their students' welfare above all else

Figure 11.18.   Qualities of a Good Principal

CHAPTER 11 INSTANT REPLAY: THE SECRETS OF CHAMPIONS

1. Read and value books: They are a great way to help set and carry out a vision.
2. Take comfort and joy in what you do and do not expect recognition from others.
3. Keep, follow, and update to-do lists.
4. Value those with whom you work regularly.
5. Be sincere and truthful with yourself and others.
6. Think and plan ahead.
7. Build and maintain relationships with your principal colleagues, as they are where you find inspiration.
8. Do not be afraid to trade your perfect grey suit for a bandanna every now and then.
9. Practice balance.
10. Relish your job; the opportunity to lead is a true gift.

BIBLIOGRAPHY

Aegerter, L. (2000, April). *Matrix of identity*. Paper presented at the meeting of the American Educational Research Association, Seattle, Wash.

Aesop, McGovern, A., & Geisert, A. (1963). *Aesop's fables*. New York: Scholastic.

Ambrose, S. (1997). *Undaunted courage: Meriwether Lewis, Thomas Jefferson, and the opening of the American west*. New York: Simon & Schuster.

The American Heritage Dictionary, 4th ed. (2000). New York: Houghton Mifflin.

Angelou, M. (1983). *I know why the caged bird sings*. New York: Bantam Books.

Barnard, C. (1940). *The functions of the executive*. Cambridge, Mass.: Harvard University Press.

Bauer, S., & Bogotch, I. (1997). *An analysis of the relationships between site council resources, council practices, and outcomes*. (ERIC Document Reproduction Service No. ED 415262)

Berliner, D., & Biddle B. (1996). *The manufactured crisis*. New York: Addison Wesley.

Bruno, J. (1997). *It's about time: Leading school reform in an era of time scarcity*. Thousand Oaks, Calif.: Corwin Press.

Conway, J., & Calz, F. (1995, December/1996, January). The dark side of shared decision making. *Educational Leadership, 53*, 45–49.

Cummins J., & Swain, M. (1989). *Bilingualism in education: Aspects of theory, research, and practice*. Boston: Addison Wesley.

Dale, G., & Janssen, J. (2001). *The seven secrets of successful coaches*. Oregon, Ill.: Quality Books, Inc.

Danielson, C. (1996). *Enhancing professional practice: A framework for teaching.* New York: ASCD.

David, J. (1995, December/1996, January). The who, what, and why of site-based management. *Educational Leadership, 53,* 4–9.

Davis, A. (1983). *Women, race, and class.* New York: Random House.

De Becker, G. (1998). *The gift of fear.* New York: Dell.

Delpit, L. (1996). *Other people's children: Cultural conflict in the classroom.* New York: New Press.

Dinesen, I. (1992). *Out of Africa.* New York: Modern Library.

Ellis, J. (1998). *American sphinx: The character of Thomas Jefferson.* New York: Knopf.

Elmore, R. (1999). *Distributive leadership.* New York: Teachers College Press.

Ferriss, S. (1998). *The fight in the fields: Cesar Chavez and the farm workers movement.* New York: Harvest Books.

Frost, R. (1920). *Mountain interval.* New York: Henry Holt and Co.

Heaphy, M., & Gruska, G. (1995). *The Malcolm Baldrige National Quality Award: A yardstick for quality.* New York: Prentice Hall.

Heisler, M. (1996). *They shoot coaches, don't they? UCLA and the NCAA since John Wooden.* New York: Hungry Minds, Inc.

Herrnstein, R., & Murray, C. (1999). *The bell curve: Intelligence and class structure in American life.* New York: Free Press.

Hertz, J. C. (1997). *Joystick nation.* New York: Little, Brown & Co.

Hess, H., Neugroshel, J., & Freedman, R. (2003). *Siddhartha: An Indian tale.* New York: Penguin.

Hoff, B. (1983). *The tao of Pooh.* New York: Viking Press.

Hoff, B. (1993). *The te of Piglet.* New York: Viking Press.

Housden, R. (2001). *Ten poems to change your life.* New York: Harmony Books.

Houseman, A. E. (1896). *A Shropshire lad.* London: Kegan, Paul, Trench, Traurere, and Co.

Hugo, V. (1998). *Les miserables.* New York: Pocket Books.

Iacocca, L., & Novak, W. (1986). *Iacocca: An autobiography.* New York: Bantam Books.

Ibani, I. (2000). *Nike yesterday and today: A fulcrum of Nike history.* New York: Random House.

Jackson, S. (1982). *The lottery and other short stories.* New York: Noonday Press.

Johnston, F., Jones, M., & Corrin, K. (1998). *Book buddies.* New York: Guilford Press.

Kennedy, C. (2003). *A patriot's handbook.* New York: Hyperion.

Kovalik, S. (1993). *ITI: The model integrated thematic instruction.* Los Angeles: Discovery Press.

Lazenby, R. (2001). *Mindgames: Phil Jackson's long strange journey.* New York: McGraw-Hill.

Lee, H. (1988). *To kill a mockingbird.* New York: Little, Brown, & Co.

Levey, J., & Acker-Hocevar, M. (1998). *Site-based management: Retrospective understandings and future directions.* (ERIC Document Reproduction Service No. ED 428439)

Lindbergh, A. (1957). *Gift from the sea.* New York: Pantheon Books.

Luft, J. (1970). *Group process: An introduction to group dynamics.* New York: National Press Books.

Mager, R. (1997). *Preparing instructional objectives.* Atlanta, Ga.: The Center for Effective Performance.

McCloskey, W., Mikow-Porto, V., & Bingham, S. (1998). *Reflecting on progress: Site-based management and school improvement in North Carolina.* (ERIC Document Reproduction Service No. ED 421766)

McLean, R. (1998). *Zen fables for today.* New York: Avon Books.

Melville, H. (2003). *White jacket.* Wickford, R.I.: North Books.

Odden, E., & Wohlstetter, P. (1995, February). Making school-based management work. *Educational Leadership, 52,* 32–36.

Papson, S., & Founder, R. (2000). *Nike culture.* New York: Random House.

Pipher, M. (1995). *Reviving Ophelia: Saving the selves of adolescent girls.* New York: Ballantine Books.

Plath, S. (2000). *The bell jar.* New York: Perennial.

Pressley, M. (2002). *Reading instruction that works.* New York: Guilford Press.

Quindlen, A. (1998). *How reading changed my life.* New York: Random House.

Rand, A. (2002). *The fountainhead.* New York: Plume.

Reeves, D. (2001). *Making standards work.* Denver, Colo.: Advanced Learning Press.

Schlecty, P. (1997). *Inventing better schools.* San Francisco: Jossey-Bass.

Schmoker, M. (2004). *Results: The key to continuous school improvement.* New York: ASCD.

Sergiovanni, T. (1992). *Moral leadership.* San Francisco: Jossey-Bass.

Seuss, Dr. (1960). *Green eggs and ham.* New York: Random House.

Silverstein, S. (1964). *The giving tree.* New York: Harper Collins.

Spring, J. (2001). *Conflict of interests: The politics of American education.* New York: McGraw-Hill.

Tapscott, D. (1999). *Growing up digital.* New York: McGraw-Hill.

Tealander, R. (2001, March 22). The literary Lakers. *The Chicago Sun Times,* S3.

Thoreau, H. D. (1995). *Walden.* Boston: Houghton Mifflin.

Tomlinson, C. A. (1999). *The differentiated classroom.* New York: ASCD.

Tooms, A. (2003). A field guide to surviving the principalship. *Principal,* 42 (3), 33–40.

Tooms, A. (January, 2005). Have you met my friend Robert? The power of the right book at the right time. *Program Resources.*

Waller, W. (1938). *The sociology of teaching.* Cambridge, Mass.: Harvard Press.

Welch, J. (2001). *Jack: Straight from the gut.* New York: Warner Books.

Wells, R. (1992a). *The divine secrets of the ya-ya sisterhood.* New York: Harper Collins.

Wells, R. (1992b). *Little altars everywhere.* New York: HarperCollins.

Wong, H. (2001). *The first days of school: How to be an effective teacher.* Mountain View, Calif.: Harry K. Wong Publications.

Yaeger, D. (2004). *Lou Holtz & Notre Dame: Deception under the golden dome.* New York: HarperCollins.

INDEX

ABOUT THE AUTHOR

Autumn Tooms is an assistant professor of K–12 educational administration in the Department of Teaching, Leadership, and Curriculum
Studies. Dr. Tooms joined the faculty at Kent State in August of 2001 after serving as a school administrator for eight years in Phoenix, Arizona.
She has worked primarily in large 1,000–3,000 student urban core
schools that serve at-risk and culturally diverse populations. Her contributions as an administrator include desegregating a school, implementing a schoolwide dual language acquisition program, and restructuring
school curricula to increase standardized test scores. Her primary areas
of inquiry center on induction and training of new principals and how
the principal can best serve as curriculum leader.